Praise for *Story Des*

"Finally. A fresh take on design-driven innovation that is simple, practical and human . . . because it is grounded in the 'untapped superpower' we all share: narrative intelligence. Fusing domain expertise from the worlds of documentary storytelling and design science, Denise Withers has produced a powerful yet pragmatic guide to solving even the most complex of problems, using an agile approach that keeps people front and center. Easy to read, full of helpful tools and illustrative anecdotes, this is a valuable resource for innovation practitioners, corporate strategists, change agents and any group or organization that is struggling with the challenge of turning its trajectory in a dynamic and uncertain environment."

LARA LEE
President, Orchard Supply Hardware (division of Lowe's Companies, Inc.)

"Design is the current innovation buzzword in government and non-profit. But design is long, hard and often thankless and fruitless work—especially when you have zero resources. *Story Design* will help you develop and make the most of your innate ability to tell stories as innovation quests. Denise Withers shows you how to stay inspired and inspire others, with practical tools and tips to design for real change."

JERRY KOH
Director of Systems Innovation & MaRS Solutions Lab, MaRS Discovery District

"*Story Design* demonstrates that narrative—one of our oldest and most meaningful ways of communicating, of enlisting collaborators to solve problems—is as effective in the modern workplace as it was around the nomadic campfire. As I read, I could visualize our ancestors using similar processes to discover how to ignite the first fire, develop primitive tools and move from caves into built structures. *Story Design* provides a template for innovating by design and learning to articulate the problems that need to be solved, so that we can forge ahead with confidence in our methods—even when the outcome is uncertain."

WHITNEY JOHNSON
Thinkers50; critically acclaimed author of *Disrupt Yourself*

"While the need for innovation in all areas of human endeavor is undisputed, the 'how to' of innovation still remains a mystery to most. *Story Design* provides a useful guidebook for the innovation process by tapping into the human ability to understand and create stories. The book uses familiar language and structures to lead you, the hero of the innovation story, from problem definition to resolution. Your innovation adventure awaits."

ANTHONY WOLF
Vice President, Product Development and Innovation, Canadian Tire Corporation

STORY DESIGN

Denise Withers

STORY
DESIGN

The
Creative
Way to
Innovate

nlab

the nlab
www.denisewithers.com
Vancouver BC

ISBN 978-1-7750559-0-7 (paperback)
ISBN 978-1-7750559-1-4 (ebook)

Produced by Page Two
www.pagetwostrategies.com
Cover design by Peter Cocking
Interior design by Naomi MacDougall
Illustrations by Michelle Clement

17 18 19 20 21   5 4 3 2 1

For my mother, who showed me the beauty of smart, strong women.

"Creativity requires the courage to let go of certainties."

—ERICH FROMM

CONTENTS

Preface

GENOMIC RESEARCHERS WORK at the jagged front edge of innovation, creating breakthroughs every day that change the fate of our species and our planet. Yet one of the toughest things about their job isn't the science—it's dealing with research grants. Developing logic models, writing proposals, managing projects, evaluating outcomes and crafting impact stories all suck up precious research time—and make most scientists see red—tape, that is. That's why one of my university clients asked me to design a way to make the burden of bureaucracy more manageable. I've worked with academics for years and know that researchers at this level are extremely busy, businesslike and brilliant. My solution would have to be easy to learn and apply immediately.

So, I put a couple of two-hour story design workshops together for half a dozen of Canada's top scientists. The idea was to show them how they could use a simple story model to construct (or design) a research project proposal for funders. The model would enable them to test out their ideas to make sure their logic and proposed outcomes were sound. Then, once their research was complete, they could use the same story model to deconstruct (or analyze) what had happened during the project. By comparing the before-and-after project stories, they could quickly evaluate their achievements and identify future research opportunities.

Since it's easier to learn to tell stories about things that have already happened than it is to imagine future stories, I used the first workshop to show the scientists how to use the model to record the story of a past project. They quickly saw how simple it was to evaluate progress, identify innovation opportunities and report on achievements. As a bonus, they also discovered that this approach gave them a ready-to-use impact story to share with stakeholders.

At the end of the first workshop, I asked them to do a bit of homework and sketch the story of a recently completed project for practice. My plan was to use the second workshop the following morning to show them how to use the model to design future research stories and proposals.

When they returned the next day, I asked them how their homework had gone. "Terrible," one guy snapped. Surprised, I asked what had happened. A true innovator, he had decided to skip ahead and try using the story logic model to sketch out a multimillion-dollar research project he was planning to submit to a European funding agency. As the future story of his proposal took shape, he quickly discovered flaws in the logic of his research design and realized that his original idea wasn't going to work. He'd have to iterate—try something different. "So, by 'terrible,' you mean it was great, right? Because an investment of twenty minutes just saved you from wasting six years and millions of dollars on a project doomed to fail." His peers laughed, and he grudgingly agreed.

Positioning his project as a springboard, I then helped the group learn to sketch, test and share future projects. By the end of the second workshop, every scientist in the room knew how to use story as a logic model to design, assess and report on research projects. Even better, they were all able to tell me the one-minute impact story of their current or future projects—a critical skill in any industry.

Though this isn't the biggest or most famous story design project I've completed, I chose it to kick off this book for three reasons. First, the fact that a scientist new to story design was able to figure out how to use my model to plan his project, in just a few minutes, demonstrates how easy the process is to learn and apply. The fact that the darn thing worked, saving him precious time and making his innovation better, demonstrates that it generates real, immediate value. And the fact that I was able to help the world's best researchers learn to share their impact stories to spread their innovations more broadly demonstrates to me that this work has real potential to change the way we design for the future.

The Back Story

I wrote this book in response to client requests to make my tools and expertise available to those who can't work with me directly. It's a great fit with my personal mission: to find creative ways to mobilize our collective wisdom to tackle the planet's most complex problems. I spent the first twenty years of my career making TV documentaries, researching and sharing breakthrough scientific and social stories—from experiments with the first genetically modified organisms (GMOs) to the spread of human immunodeficiency virus (HIV) in sub-Saharan Africa. I learned about people, politics and purpose. Most importantly, I learned sense-making: how to use my narrative intelligence to analyze and resolve complex problems through the lens of story.

Life as a filmmaker was grand until the turn of the century when reality TV hit, backed up over and dragged the North American documentary market to a melodramatic, messy death. Like many people, organizations and industries in recent years, I lost my livelihood almost overnight. Devastated, I had no choice but to look for a new career—to pivot, as the cool kids say.

With an eye on the future of digital media, I went to grad school to study narrative and design as part of the first cohort in the School of Interactive Arts and Technology at Simon Fraser University in Surrey, British Columbia. For two years I camped out in a makeshift design lab, buried in the back of an old Walmart. (Our new campus was still just a sketch.) There, I did a deep dive into cognitive psychology, intelligence, engagement and learning theory. As I unpacked and compared these concepts, I discovered that the work I'd been doing as a filmmaker for two decades was really a form of design—or problem-solving. I'd been using story as a way to solve communication and education problems. I had been designing stories to change beliefs and behavior.

Through this research, I started to develop an emerging theory of narrative intelligence, connecting traditional design and problem-solving methods to our innate abilities to use story for analysis, learning and innovation. It was the first time I started to think about story as something more than a communication tool, something we all might be able to use to change the way we research and design solutions to complex problems. Though it was fascinating work, I couldn't imagine how I could use it to make a living.

When I finished my studies, a local business school recruited me to lead new initiatives in curriculum innovation. Once I got down to work there, I was stunned to discover that basic problem-solving was not part of the program—even though it had become one of the top three skills demanded by today's employers. Like other business schools, the faculty taught ad hoc analytical tools such as SWOT (strengths, weaknesses, opportunities and threats) analysis and the blue ocean strategy. But none of the schools taught a methodical process to help students learn to define real-world problems clearly—then research, design, test and refine solutions that worked.

A colleague and I saw this curriculum gap as an opportunity and spent the next couple of years developing and launching a studio for strategic design at the university—the first of its kind in Canada. Our program introduced learners to a generic design process, similar to what they would experience at Stanford. Though students of all ages liked the idea of a hands-on problem-solving method, they still struggled to master the generic approach and ad hoc suite of tools in just one semester.

Once the studio was up and running, I left the university to work as an innovation and engagement consultant. That's when I started to experiment with story as a framework for design. My hunch was that story design would be easier for my clients to learn and use than other design processes because it's grounded in cognitive structures and systems that humans already know and understand. It's natural and intuitive. Most other design methods are too abstract, which makes them hard for people to remember unless they use them every day. And my hunch was right. Clients who tried my story design approach loved it and were able to use it right away.

Over the past few years, I've developed a suite of story tools, including the Story Specs™ and the Story Canvas™, to help clients apply and share the story design process with their teams. I'm publishing this book to share that same story design for innovation goodness with you—to help you learn to use your untapped narrative intelligence to bring your big ideas to life.

Whew! So that's how we got here. Now—let's go!

Introduction

This is NOT a book about story telling.

Story Design is a playbook for story-powered innovation. It's a how-to book that brings the power and process of creatives like filmmakers to leaders like you. To help you go beyond story telling and learn to use story as a design tool. To innovate. Turn ideas into action. Develop your next big thing. And engage others in your quest.

This book shows you how to take the process that authors use to design stories and put it to work to research and design all kinds of other things—from projects and experiences to campaigns and strategies.

I know, I know. There are hundreds of books on story telling and thousands of experts teaching story courses. So, what's the X-factor here? What makes this book extraordinary?

This is the only book that teaches you how to design and innovate by channeling a superpower you already have: narrative intelligence. What's that? It's something that we're born with, that we all share. Something that goes far beyond simply telling stories.

Narrative intelligence (NI) is the way humans think, learn, analyze and remember experiences and information. It's our innate ability to make sense of and solve complex problems through the lens of story. It's the foundation of our analytic and creative skills. Our natural design process. It's an underdeveloped superpower with incredible potential—like a hidden core muscle we don't flex often enough.

NI is what enables you to turn on a TV show when it's half over and figure out what's happening. Analyze past behavior of a competitor and predict her next move. Imagine the future and design a technology to make it real. Listen to customers describe a problem and zero in on the root cause. Laugh at a joke before the punch line because you know what's coming. Cry when Simba loses his father and your heart breaks for him.

Narrative intelligence isn't new. Neither is design. But no one has ever put them together before to reveal their untapped potential. This book works a bit like a narrative intelligence boot camp to help you go beyond story telling and fire up your NI muscles—to give you the hands-on tools you need to start thinking and working like a designer. So that you can discover how to use story as a platform for innovation—right here, right now.

This book has two parts.

PART ONE: HOW STORY DESIGN WORKS

This section introduces the three key concepts that drive story design: story, narrative intelligence and design. Using the Story Specs™ as a model, Part One shows you what each one is, how it works and why you need all three to design for innovation.

PART TWO: HOW TO DO STORY DESIGN

Part Two brings your big ideas to life with the Story Canvas™—a planning tool that gets you working like a designer. It'll help you strengthen your NI muscles, so that you can use them to research and design innovative content, experiences and strategies that move people, on purpose.

Both the Story Specs and the Story Canvas are agile tools that you can learn to use in a few minutes—and continue to use for the rest of your life.

Who needs story design?

Anyone with a dream. Anyone who loves discovery. Anyone who can't resist a dare. Anyone struggling to define a vision for a better future. Anyone with a mandate for innovation. Which is basically everyone these days!

And that's a problem. Because most of us never had the opportunity to learn what innovation is, why it matters or how to do it. We just know that when we don't do it, or mess it up, we get yelled at—or worse.

I decided to write this book specifically for all of you who are under pressure to innovate—or else. Because I want you to succeed. I want you to have a safe way to start to innovate right now. To have creative tools and techniques that you can use anywhere, anytime to research, design, test and refine new ideas. An easy-to-use approach that costs nothing to put into practice. A new way to study, shape and share your next big thing that is completely risk-free.

I decided to write this book because I do know what innovation is and I do know how to do it. I also know that story design can make it easy for you.

WHY DO YOU NEED TO INNOVATE?

When I start to work with new clients, I always ask them why they want to innovate. Because figuring out *why* is the toughest—and most important—part of the process. It is The Beginning. You have to determine what problem you need to solve and why it matters before you can start to work on a solution. Think of innovation as a road trip—you need to have some idea of your desired destination before you can start to choose a route. Without fail, my clients always give me the same answer: "The status quo isn't working."

They go on to explain their situation by saying things like: "All our usual methods of problem-solving have failed"; "The problem is too big or complex"; "We don't know how or where to get started" or "We need a new way to do things."

They think that innovation is the answer because every management blog, journal and fridge magnet tells them so. Innovation is the holy grail for leaders these days. Everyone's talking about it. And everyone wants it.

Ironically, few really need it. When I use story to analyze most of my clients' problems, I typically find that they don't need innovation at all. What they do need is change.

Wait—there's a difference?

Absolutely, and it's huge. So huge that there are thousands of books published on both topics, with new ones hitting the virtual shelves every day. As this is a playbook and not a textbook, I'm not going to do a deep dive into the theory of innovation. If you want that, check out *Change by Design* by Tim Brown and Barry Katz[1] or *The Art of Innovation* by Tom Kelley.[2]

For the work you're about to do throughout this book, here's what you need to know.

When you engage in a design process to create change, you produce an outcome that is different from the status quo. At the end of the process, *something* is different from the way it was when you started. It could be behavior, knowledge, attitudes, skills, choices, values. Maybe someone bought, built or destroyed something. Went somewhere, ate something. The difference or change can be anything—big or small. If I am hungry, then eat a meal, I am not hungry anymore. My status has changed from hungry to full.

When you follow a design process to create an innovation, you produce an outcome that is not only different but also completely new to the world. That's big. Because, when you apply that definition to a lot of what is labeled "innovation," you discover that it is simply change. I hate to burst your bubble. But if you do something that is new to you or your organization and others have been doing it for years somewhere else, that is not innovation.

WHY INNOVATE INSTEAD OF CHANGE?

In many ways, change can be safer and easier than innovation. You can simply copy the changes others have made, to repeat their successes. That way, you can't fail. However, you'll also only ever be as good as those you copy. You'll never be able to lead. Get ahead. Create an advantage. Or crack open an entirely new sphere of potential. And that's okay. Change plays a valuable and important role in creating better futures.

Those who truly want to innovate do it because they know that the world is a chaotic place, evolving at dizzying speed. Their old-world ways of doing, being, acting and thinking can't help them solve dynamic, new-world kinds of problems. They know we need to get beyond incremental change. To create different—and completely new—ways to live, work and play.

In other words, figuring out whether you need change or innovation comes down to defining the problem you need to resolve. Why does this matter? It's that road trip thing again—you need to know where you're trying to go before you can figure out how to get there. Innovation is crazy hard work. Why reinvent the wheel if all you need is a tire change?

Think about it. If your problem is one that someone else has already solved, you simply need to find and adapt that solution to your own context and you're good to go. If not, if it's a wicked problem that has the world stumped, then you need to innovate.

WHAT'S STOPPING YOU?

If you already know why you need to innovate, then my next question is: What's stopping you from doing it?

"Lack of resources."

That's the number-one excuse I hear—and I don't buy it. As you'll discover throughout this playbook, constraints like limited resources actually drive innovation—they don't block it. So why is it that despite a recent tsunami of books, courses and consultants flooding the marketplace to help leaders like you navigate this tricky new space, our society still struggles to innovate?

In my experience, the barriers to innovation are all driven by the same thing: fear of failure. This shows up in many ways—in projects and practices where clients keep doing the same old things the same old ways even though they know things are broken. And in the excuses people give to avoid trying something new.

- Innovation is too risky. What if our idea doesn't work?
- It's too experimental. We need structure and deliverables.
- How can we invest in innovation when we don't know what we'll get from it?
- We can't afford to innovate.
- I'm not creative enough for this.
- I just need someone to tell me the "right" way to do it.

In other words, we lack confidence, methods for and practice in this kind of creative and ambiguous problem-solving. That's the bad news. The good news is that you're about to get all those things—and more—through this book.

How to Use This Playbook

Story design for innovation works best when you collaborate with others.

Here are a few ways you can use this book to help build design expertise in your organization and community so that you're all speaking the same language.

SHARE IT WITH YOUR TEAM BEFORE STARTING A PROJECT.

For large ventures, I'd recommend having your team read the book—then work through a test project to get everyone up to speed. Make it something fun so there's nothing to lose if they make mistakes. And make it relevant so it's meaningful enough to keep them engaged.

USE IT AS A TEXTBOOK TO TEACH INNOVATION COURSES.

I teach story design regularly to clients across sectors. The tools and methods are agile enough to adapt to just about any organization or challenge. You can use the structure of the book to create a course that you can deliver across four or more modules in a weekend or a month.

GIVE IT TO CLIENTS TO PREPARE THEM FOR UPCOMING ENGAGEMENTS.

I co-create all my design projects with my clients. So they need to have a working knowledge of story design to be effective. For the past few years, I've had to run a two-day Story School at the start of every large project to establish this foundation. Now that the playbook is done, I'll be able to share it with clients and their teams before projects launch—which will let us hit the ground running.

DISTRIBUTE IT TO YOUR STAKEHOLDERS AND COMMUNITY TO GUIDE OPEN INNOVATION.

More and more organizations are sharing knowledge and expertise openly to solve complex problems. But how do you get people from different countries and cultures to work together effectively? That's the beauty of story design. Story is a universal language. Everyone across the globe has narrative intelligence and knows how it works. By giving all the players on your innovation team this book, you can get everyone aligned in just a few hours.

What makes this story design process special?

"Innovate or die." Sound familiar? That's the sound of global innovation consultancies creating a panicked call to action for business leaders—and a nice fat market for their services. Innovation training and consulting is big business these days—a cornerstone for the multinational giants.

So why should you choose my little story design methodology over theirs?

It's simple. No, really. Story design is simple. It's actually the easiest way to learn to innovate because you already know how story works. Even better, so does everyone on your team.

That's the biggest benefit. What else does story design do for you that other methods don't?

- Creates a risk-free way to test and refine ideas anywhere, anytime.
- Provides practical design tools for anyone to use, on any kind of problem.
- Makes wicked problems bite-sized and manageable.
- Develops your creative capacity to lead through chaos and complexity.
- Ensures you solve the right problem and avoid wasting resources.

Most of all, story design helps you turn ideas into innovations faster than any other design approach. Now that you know why you need it, let's discover how it works.

Part One

How Story Design Works

▶ **The Three
Key Concepts
You Need
to Know**

THE CHAPTERS IN PART ONE take your narrative intelligence to the next level, introducing you to a story framework that will help you make sense of complex problems and design innovative solutions.

We'll jump right in with an introduction to the Story Specs model. As we explore this framework, we'll cut through all the hype about story and identify a few basic mechanics so we're all on the same page about how story works.

Next, we'll dive into the concept of narrative intelligence—the superpower behind story design—to reveal what it is, how it works and why you need it. I'll also share a few real-world examples so you can see the theory in action.

Finally, we'll explore design to debunk some myths and discover why it's essential for innovation.

In Part Two, we'll combine these three concepts for the first time and put theory into practice. You'll try some new story design tools and techniques, and learn how to use them to research and design your next innovation project.

Story Specs™
A Practical
Model

THE STORY SPECS (as in *specifications* or *spectacles*) illustrated on the next page offer a simple visual model of how story and narrative intelligence work. I originally developed this framework as a way to teach introductory story structure. Over the years, it has evolved into a deceptively powerful tool that now helps my clients make sense of, learn from and design solutions to complex challenges—all through the lens of story.

Here's how story works in this model.

At the start of every story, a hero runs into a *problem* that she can't solve. She then goes off on a *quest* for knowledge, skills or resources to help her design a *resolution*. At the end, she figures it out, gives up or dies trying!

In other words, *a story simply describes how a hero solves a problem.*

Hold on—that's it? What about the hero's journey? Eight-step process? Inciting incident? Crisis? Climax? Protagonist? Setting?

Those are all elements of epic story design. And if you're creating a novel or screenplay, you might want to explore them later. Or read *Story: Substance, Structure, Style, and the Principles of Screenwriting* by Robert

McKee—it's easily the best book for those who want to learn the intricacies of classic story telling.[1]

The Story Specs simplify things to represent the essence of story—from a narrative intelligence perspective. They're distilled from centuries of classic and modern story theory and informed by my thirty-five years of research and practice using story for sense-making and problem-solving. After working across sectors, media and genres, I discovered that this story model is all you really need to use story as a design framework for innovation.

So let's unpack the Story Specs to get a better look at its key concepts and mechanics.

Story

Ask a group of story tellers to define *story* and you're bound to start a fight. No one has come up with a definition that works for everyone.

As a side note, learning to live with ambiguity is a key skill for designers. If not having "the" correct definition or answer to a question drives you crazy, you may have some work to do before going much further in this book. Check out *Creative Confidence: Unleashing the Creative Potential Within Us All* by the Kelley brothers from IDEO as an excellent starting point to help you open up to the uncertainty inherent in innovation.[2]

My definitions of the key elements of story are working concepts that I use in my practice. Love 'em or leave 'em. My goal is simply to give you tools that work for you. Feel free to adapt them to your own needs.

Earlier, I wrote that every story describes how a hero solves a problem. Specifically, it describes *the experience* of a hero as she solves a problem. Different story theorists use different language to describe the problem concept, including *dramatic conflict, tension, imbalance, gap.* I'll use *problem* in this book, defined loosely as any sort of unresolved challenge, goal, need, opportunity or question.

If we break down this story definition into its basic parts, it looks like this:

Story = Problem + Quest + Resolution

Simple, right? If you think about it, it works. Try it out. This structure fits every story you've ever encountered.

- **Harry Potter.** The young wizard has to kill Lord Voldemort. So he goes on a quest to destroy the secret source of Voldemort's power (his horcruxes), which weakens him to the point of death.

- **The Lord of the Rings.** Frodo the hobbit has to destroy the ring of power. So he journeys through the dangers of Mordor to cast the ring into the fires of Mount Doom.

- **The Hunger Games.** Katniss Everdeen has to save her family and her people from the tyranny of Panem. So she leads a rebellion to overthrow the Capitol city.

- **Climate Smart.** Leaders at Ecotrust Canada want to help small businesses cut greenhouse gases and save money. So they develop a training program, which they sell through a new social enterprise.

- **B Corporations.** Social entrepreneurs and impact investors in the United States need a new way to create shared value. So they work with government to create a new kind of legal corporation.

- **Participle.** Change agents in the United Kingdom want to empower seniors and reform care. So they engage with community to develop the Circle Movement, a new kind of online service for care.

As you can see, each one of these stories has a problem, a quest and a resolution. Of course, you can stretch out the telling of the stories, but their essence remains the same.

What's that? You know stories that don't have problems? Can't be. Either you can't identify the problem—that is, you can't make sense of a complex mess of information to figure out what's going on, which means your narrative intelligence muscles really do need some toning up—or it's not a story.

How can that be? "There are stories everywhere! Everything I read is a story!" Here's your first tip—just because a marketer tells you her content is a story doesn't mean that it is. In fact, most content is not a story. Shocking, I know.

Let's take a quick peek at what story is *not*.

Story is *not* a description of a thing, person, service, product or organization. Not a slogan or picture. Not a tweet, snap, vine, YouTube video, PowerPoint slide show, spreadsheet, infographic. In fact, technology cannot generate stories. (Yes, another marketing hype busted.) Stories must be deliberately designed by a story designer—a human, as of this writing. Online tools and systems can generate content— bits of text, images and sounds—but they can't yet synthesize ideas into a complete story with a problem, quest and resolution.

The easiest way to determine whether something is a story is to find the problem. That is the heart and soul of the story—the engine that drives it from beginning to end. No problem—no story. You'll start to see how this works better in the next few sections.

Narrative

People often get confused about the difference between narrative and story. As I mentioned, I can't give you the absolute definition for either—I can just tell you what I've learned that works for me.

In the last section, I said that each story describes *one specific experience* of a hero as she attempts to resolve a specific problem. In the Story Specs, the hero's experience is represented by the quest. The quest includes a series of little dots, sometime called *story beats*. Each beat typically represents one specific action by the hero—one specific attempt to try to resolve the problem.

In contrast, a narrative represents *a collection of related stories*, typically unfolding over time. For example, the Apollo 11 moon landing is one specific story that brings to life the narrative of space exploration. In this way, a narrative is like an ongoing TV series, which is made up of individual story episodes.

However, a narrative is bigger than a collection of individual stories. If you think about stories occurring at ground level—on the earth's surface—then a narrative sits at thirty thousand feet. Now, imagine you're flying over the earth at that height. You can't see all the details of every single house, tree and person. But you can see clusters or patterns of things that help you make sense of the landscape. Green blobs snaked with blue ribbons. Dense collections of light. Dark green masses. Brown squares bisected by gray grids. When you see these patterns, your brain starts to analyze what it's seeing, comparing it against other patterns and information stored in your memory. You start to identify different features. A river valley. A city at night. The rainforest. The prairies. Once you can identify these formations, you're able to assume certain details about them. There are fish in the river. The city is loud. The rainforest is cool. The fields grow wheat.

Narrative works in a similar way. When you mentally fly up to thirty thousand feet to consider a collection of stories, your brain starts to analyze them, looking for patterns. This is sense-making, your narrative intelligence at work. It's something we do automatically, unconsciously, constantly. As intelligent beings, we need to

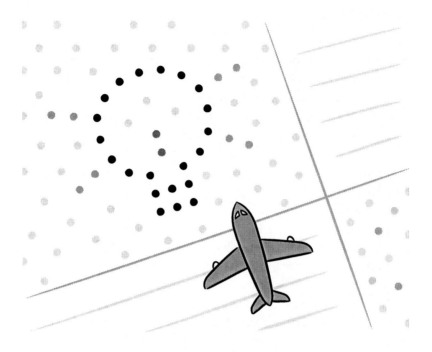

understand what's going on in the big picture of our world. How are the stories in the narrative related? What problems did their heroes resolve? How did they do it? What can we learn from those stories? And most importantly, what does it all mean to me?

This ongoing pattern analysis is the way we learn and develop expertise. From a design and innovation perspective, it's also the way we discover new bits of intel and insight that inspire breakthrough ideas—and drive us to create better futures. We'll explore narrative intelligence more deeply a bit later.

So, a narrative describes a series of related stories—and makes visible the big-picture patterns or concepts that tie those stories together. In contrast, a story takes one tiny piece of that high-level, often abstract idea and makes it real, tangible and specific through a hero's actions and experience. For example, all the stories in the narrative of space exploration share the vague concepts of risk, adventure, curiosity and discovery. The specific story of Neil Armstrong's experience during his moon walk in 1969 brings those concepts to life in a way that is easy for us to remember and share.

That's one reason why story is such a powerful leadership tool. If you're struggling to communicate the big idea in your organizational purpose, you can use a specific story to bring your narrative or purpose to life and demonstrate how it works in the real world. That specific story then becomes something employees can understand, relate to, share and build upon.

For example, Lowe's, the home improvement retailer, sponsors Habitat for Humanity Women Build, a program that teaches construction skills to women so they can help build homes for families in need. Each year, it tells the story of the projects it completed that year—for example, building an accessible home for a family whose son was paralyzed in a car accident. This story is a specific example of Lowe's purpose in action: helping people love where they live. It influences the company's culture and forms part of the organizational narrative.

The cool thing about the Story Specs model is that you can use it to work with both specific stories and big-picture narratives at any level you like. You can show the problem, quest and resolution of one tiny moment in a story—like when Neil Armstrong first steps out of the *Eagle* onto the moon. Or you can use the individual dots in the quest arc to represent all the specific stories that led up to and followed that one moment in the space exploration narrative. By zooming in and out of the dots in the model, you can use the Story Specs to share big and small ideas and experiences.

As you expand and contract the Story Specs, you will also start to see how the hero's problem in a story or narrative shifts and evolves, depending on your point of view. The problem for the big-picture space exploration narrative might be defined as finding a way for humans to live somewhere else in the solar system. In the Apollo 11 story, Neil Armstrong's problem might be defined as leading his crew to complete the first moon landing safely. That's one specific story or step that makes up part of the larger narrative; "a leap for mankind."

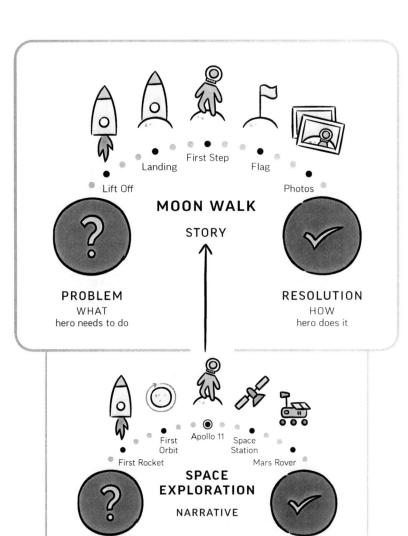

MOON WALK

Lift Off · Landing · First Step · Flag · Photos

STORY

PROBLEM
WHAT
hero needs to do

RESOLUTION
HOW
hero does it

SPACE
EXPLORATION

First Rocket · First Orbit · Apollo 11 · Space Station · Mars Rover

NARRATIVE

PROBLEM
WHAT
hero needs to do

RESOLUTION
HOW
hero does it

Trigger

Another way in which a narrative and a story are different is that a narrative tends to be open-ended and ongoing, whereas each story has a beginning, middle and end.

In the Story Specs model on page 14, the trigger marks the beginning of a specific story. The trigger is the "inciting incident" you learned about in high school, the "call to adventure" in Joseph Campbell's hero's journey, the critical story element that forces the hero into action.[3] Triggers are unexpected events that throw the hero's world out of balance. They can be big or small—anything, really. The hero could stub her toe on a hidden fossil. Get fired from her job. Discover a new chemical. Or read a provocative memo.

Going back to epic movies, we see Frodo inherit a ring of power, the Capitol reap Katniss's little sister for the Hunger Games and a tornado hit Dorothy's home. In the real world, disruptive triggers force companies to innovate all the time. Digital images killed many film companies. Email decimated postal services. Whatever the trigger is, it must be compelling enough to force the hero to respond. To take action to sort things out, seek balance and resolve the situation. Not reacting to the trigger is not an option for the hero.

In the Story Specs model, we can see that the trigger doesn't just kick off the story—it actually sets up the main problem that will drive the hero's quest until the resolution.

Problem

Understanding how the problem works in this model is essential to both story design and innovation. If you get nothing else from this book, get this!

In theory, the problem concept is pretty straightforward. As we just learned, when a trigger occurs, it disrupts the hero's world. Triggers are, by definition, unexpected. Surprises. That means that when they happen, they create a "gap" or a "disconnect" between what a hero expects to happen and what really occurs. I stop at a red light in my car and the car behind me crashes into me. Boom. I didn't expect that to happen. Instead, I expected the car behind me to stop. When it didn't, it was a total surprise. It opened a gap between my expectation and reality. As a result, my world is now disrupted, out of balance.

When we (or the hero) encounter an imbalance or gap like this that has been created by a trigger, we react—usually quickly and spontaneously. We try to close the gap and restore balance to the situation as quickly and easily as possible. If we succeed, things go back to "normal" and the story is over. I get out and check my car for damage. If there's no damage and I'm not hurt, I get back in and drive away.

If we fail in our first attempt and the gap remains open—things remain unbalanced—then we have a problem. Not just any problem but one so compelling that we (the hero) cannot rest until it is resolved. It consumes us.

This problem plays two essential, related roles in story design.

1. It defines the specific goal of the hero's quest.
2. It engages the audience.

Defining the goal for the quest is critical for any kind of design or innovation project. This is something I emphasize throughout the book. You have to know what problem you face before you start out on the quest for a solution. This sounds so obvious that it feels silly to write. But figuring this out can be desperately tricky, both in real life and in stories. In fact, clearly identifying the problem can be much harder than finding a solution. Because problems are rarely obvious or clear-cut, especially when we're caught up in the middle of them.

The trigger rarely represents the real problem—it's typically a symptom or an indicator. It's the first sign that things are out of whack. When we react by trying to resolve the imbalance created by the trigger, we often discover that the actual problem is much bigger, hairier and more complex that we thought.

It's easiest to see and study these kinds of ill-defined problems in epic stories like *The Lord of the Rings*. When Frodo starts out, he thinks he "just" has to get the ring of power to the village of Bree. By the end of the third movie, he realizes that he has to destroy the ring—at any cost—including his life. Katniss thinks she "just" needs to win one round of the Hunger Games to save her family. Later, she realizes that she must defeat the entire Panem oligarchy to set her people free. Here are a few other examples of epic Western stories and their real problems:

- ***Romeo and Juliet:*** Two lovers need to escape their family feud.
- ***Star Wars:*** Luke has to crush the Galactic Empire.
- ***Beauty and the Beast:*** Belle has to help the world learn to love.
- ***The Matrix:*** Neo has to save Zion and his people.

Once you start to look for them, spotting problems in fictional stories becomes easy. In real life, however, figuring out the actual problem is usually much harder—so we often avoid doing it. Don't. You'll find out why in Chapter 4.

Quest

Once we've figured out what our story problem is—or, at least, the first part of the problem—we can start our quest for new knowledge, skills or other stuff that will help us resolve it. The quest can be physical, emotional, cognitive or even virtual. It might help to think of the quest as a journey the hero undertakes to answer an important QUESTion.

As you're now starting to realize, at the beginning of many stories, the hero may not be able to define the problem she needs to resolve clearly. So, she responds to the trigger and starts to seek out what seems to be the most obvious resolution. That's human nature. If and when that doesn't work, she is forced to try something different, usually more difficult. As the solution continues to elude her, she has to iterate in her problem-solving. That means her quest is made up of a series of actions and reactions—the story beats that make up the quest in the Story Specs.

The hero's quest continues as long as her problem remains unsolved. Depending on the nature of your project or story, the quest could have just one story beat—or a billion. We'll dive more into the dynamics of the quest in Part Two.

RESOLUTION
HOW
hero does it

Resolution

The resolution is the outcome of the quest. It's the ultimate "thing" the hero makes, does or discovers that enables her to resolve her problem. It might be tangible or intangible. Frodo fights to the death with his nemesis, ultimately casting Gollum and the evil ring into the fires of Mount Doom. Harry Potter and his friends destroy Voldemort's horcruxes and turn his dark magic against him.

In real-world innovation stories, the resolution can be anything from a product or service to a strategy or experience. The solution to your problem could be a solar-powered jet pack, a virtual beach holiday or corporate expansion into pet therapy. It could even be a story, like a TV ad about a lost puppy and the ponies that save it.

Sounds pretty straightforward, right? It is—in hindsight. But here's the thing.

The resolution to an innovation problem is never obvious at the beginning of the project. When you set out on your innovation journey, you set out to tackle a complex problem that does not have a known resolution. That's the very nature of innovation. The great thing about this is that the resolution you ultimately produce to resolve the problem will be different and new. It will have immediate and real value (assuming you are solving a real problem).

The flip side is that the quest to find that resolution will have to be just as different and new. As the saying goes, "If you always do what you've always done, you'll always get what you've always got." That means your innovation journey will also be hard. Following someone else's footsteps is easy. Bushwhacking a new trail is not.

If you want to produce a resolution that is truly innovative, you have to do the work. Spend time defining the problem accurately. Commit to the quest. Get out of your comfort zone and slay all the dragons. Climb all the mountains. Battle all the bad guys. And stay on task right until the end to make sure your resolution will work. That means no shortcuts. No cheating or assumptions. No flipping to the last page of the book. If your hero resolves her problem on the first try, you don't have much of a story. The same is true for innovation. No risk—no reward.

What's worse than all that slogging? Not knowing when or how it will end.

It's funny. When we're consuming a story, in the movie theater or curled up with a book, not knowing how the quest will end keeps us engaged, on the hook. Most of us love the suspense of a thriller. Sustained dramatic tension is the sign of great story design.

In real life, though, we can't stand this kind of suspense. Most of us hate the idea of starting a project and not knowing what the resolution will be—what we're going to produce or how our own quest will turn out. We're very uncomfortable with this kind of ambiguity—and naturally risk-averse. That's why we always want to leap to a solution—why we dislike spending time exploring and defining the problem, testing ideas. We'd much rather assume that we know the problem and solution and just get on with it already!

Unfortunately, this aversion to uncertainty is one of the biggest barriers to innovation. My research shows that one of the keys to engaging people in any kind of problem-solving is to give them clear, achievable goals.[4] Innovation can feel like the opposite of that—which is why it's so difficult to get people to commit to it. No one wants to work on something that feels pointless. No one wants to join a quest that makes her feel lost in the wilderness, that lacks a clear destination. We want to know what we're trying to achieve—and why it matters.

That's where the last part of the Story Specs comes in.

Purpose

PURPOSE
WHY
it matters

What keeps Frodo going when he runs out of hope and all seems lost? What drives Harry Potter to risk his life again and again to defeat Voldemort? Why does Rocky keep getting in that damned boxing ring to get his face smashed in?

Purpose.

When a hero—or innovator—is in the middle of a quest, she can't see the finish line. She doesn't know what the resolution to the problem is—or if she'll even find one. But she does know why she has to keep going—why she can't give up. She has something that drives her above all: a purpose.

Purpose is your raison d'être. It describes the reason you're doing this work. The impact you want to have, the thing you ultimately want to change through your story design, through your innovation. As an innovator or a leader, you have to know why you need to resolve your problem if you want to succeed. And you must be able to articulate your purpose if you want others to engage in your quest. We need to know why something matters in order to commit to it. Purpose is the reason a hero undertakes and is compelled to complete the quest.

Let's see this in action. Going back to *The Lord of the Rings*, Frodo's problem is finding a way to destroy the ring of power. His purpose—the reason why he has to do this or die trying—is to save the world from evil. His quest includes a series of steps toward destroying the ring. His resolution is unexpected, as he has to throw his enemy into the fire to do it. The impact of this resolution—the change created—is a world safe from evil.

No matter what you're doing, your purpose is (almost) always to create change. You want to design a thing that changes the way someone thinks, feels, acts. The way she behaves. What she values, believes, wants, does. If you succeed in your quest, something will be different afterward. If you're innovating, it will be different—and new. The change could be simple: making it easier to clean floors. Or complex: curing cancer. The result of the change you create is your impact.

For example, my purpose is to teach you to use story for innovation. My problem is to figure out the best way to do that. This book is my resolution. If you complete your quest to work through this book and do learn to use story for innovation, I will have achieved my purpose. I will have changed (improved) your innovation capacity. The impact of that will be more/better innovation in the future.

In short, as the hero of a story design for innovation quest, if you figure out how to resolve your problem, you'll achieve your purpose.

Even if you're simply telling a story, you're still doing it for a purpose: to change the listener's understanding, perception, values, knowledge, attitudes. You might want people to do something differently, to view you differently, to understand a situation differently. So, you design a story intentionally to achieve that purpose.

Hero

Hero

In simple terms, the hero is (usually) the main character in the story. Many great story tellers will argue that the hero is also the most important element in the story—that creating a complex, multilayered character is the secret to engaging audiences. I disagree. My research—and the work of others, including Aristotle and Disney[5]—shows that it's not the hero's psyche that grabs and keeps our attention. It's her actions. Her behavior. Her choices. What she actually does to resolve the problem. The decisions she makes.

I'm not going to go into much detail about how to create an intricate psychological profile of a compelling hero. If you want to learn that, again, I suggest you read Robert McKee's *Story*; he does a terrific job of explaining character development. For this kind of story design and innovation work, though, here's what you need to know.

The hero usually leads the quest. During that journey, she is forced to make choices—consciously and unconsciously—about how best to resolve the problem. Each decision she makes reveals something about her values and beliefs—and, ultimately, defines her character.

Her decisions also help us, as story consumers, identify and engage with her purpose. Great story designers don't tell you about the hero—they show you who she is through story action. As an aside, this is also true of organizations. Your brand isn't determined by your logo or what you say—it'd defined by what you do.

As the key "decision maker" in the story, the hero plays a critical role in "designing" the resolution, taking actions that determine how things will turn out. Since these actions are ultimately guided by her need to make change—her purpose—we can start to see that the hero is actually a change agent. It doesn't matter if she's pursuing personal, social, system, organizational or behavioral change. The bottom line in every story is that the hero will do something that will cause the world to be different when the story ends.

Why does this matter? Because we're here to figure out how to use story to innovate. Because when you start to do this work in Part Two, you will become the hero—the innovation designer—trying to figure out what actions will create the kind of change you need to make to realize your purpose. And how you can engage others in your quest.

The End

That's it. That's all you need to know about story structure. The entire Story Specs secret.

The trigger causes the hero to set out on a quest to find a resolution to a problem, which creates change for a purpose.

Big deal, right?

Yes, actually.

I don't know about you, but all of my innovation and consulting work ultimately focuses on creating change for some higher purpose. Designing experiences, strategies and content that get people to think, feel and act differently. It's a big deal because figuring out how to achieve change and purpose—how to create *new and different* solutions to complex problems—are top-level priorities for leaders these days.

The Story Specs is more than just a story framework; it's a model for innovation. A tool that helps us, as hero/designers, make sense of complex problems, navigate quests, discover resolutions and create change. An agile, affordable and accessible problem-solving engine that's powered by your narrative intelligence.

How does that work? Let's pop the hood on the big black box that is your brain and find out.

Narrative Intelligence
An Untapped Superpower

INALLY! WE'RE TALKING about narrative intelligence. Before we go any further, I want to remind you that this is a playbook about story design for innovation—not a textbook about the cognitive science of narrative intelligence (NI). So, we won't go too deep into the theory. Instead, we'll focus on practice—what you need to know about your NI to put it to use.

In my work, I use narrative intelligence to describe our innate human ability to make sense of and resolve complex problems through the lens of story.

At this point, NI isn't a formal field of study or recognized psychological "thing." It's a term first used by a group of grad students at the MIT Media Lab in the early 1990s who were researching what happens when you combine narrative and artificial intelligence. I stumbled across it in grad school while studying the concept of intelligence. In particular, I was intrigued by Howard Gardner's work that explores multiple forms of intelligence.[1] His idea, in simple terms, is that we have many kinds of intelligences—such as emotional, physical, musical, math and linguistic intelligences. These intelligences are a bit like natural gifts or expertise. According to Gardner, we all have different mixes of multiple intelligences, at different levels.

As you're about to find out, narrative intelligence is arguably the most powerful of all these intelligences for innovation. I'm fortunate to have been able to spend a lifetime developing mine, through my work as a filmmaker. What makes NI so exciting is that it's not unique to story professionals like me. Everyone has it—and everyone can strengthen it—including you. So let's take a look at how NI works and what you need to do to turn it into your own personal innovation superpower.

How intelligence works

If you've done any reading about concepts like intelligence quotient (IQ) or emotional intelligence quotient (EQ) , then you know that, at ground level, these different kinds of intelligence all work the same way. They all rely on a form of pattern recognition. Every time your brain encounters new information (like a sound, sight or smell), it starts to look for patterns. For example, patterns in the flow of traffic, in the weather, in a game, in cooking, in gardening, in the structure of a song. Once your brain detects a pattern (like dark low clouds on the horizon), it tries to match that against patterns you've encountered previously in life ("Hmm, looks like rain"). The better your brain gets at finding and matching patterns in a certain domain (like math, language or hockey), the more "expert" you become at something.

The good news is that pattern recognition is a form of problem-solving that we can all practice and get better at over our lifetime. In fact, we do this every day because much of our everyday behavior relies on pattern recognition. Driving a car is a great example. When you first start driving, you have to pay careful attention and think deliberately about what to do in different situations. As you get better at it—more expert—you're able to make decisions subconsciously and automatically. Your brain is able to match up the information it's receiving with patterns it has stored in memory, making decisions in just nanoseconds. Actions like turning left, emergency stops and changing lanes become "no-brainers." When you start to think about all the things you do every day, you can start to identify all kinds of other activities that use patterns and your innate expertise to make decisions and take actions.

How narrative intelligence works

Your narrative intelligence works the same way.

The basic idea behind NI is that we are exposed to information in story format from the time we are born. This repeated exposure stimulates our brain to establish and fortify neurological pathways that cause us to process incoming information through the lens of story. In other words, we learn from a young age to make sense of the world by organizing our thoughts into story patterns just like the Story Specs, complete with problems, quests and resolutions.[2]

Right. But how does that help us solve problems and innovate?

Every time you solve a problem, your brain archives your problem-solving experience in your memory in the form of a story "package." These packages form a sort of story library or database that is unique to you—something you develop from the day you're born until you die.

As you add stories to the database, your mind sorts them into categories that are meaningful to you—in much the same way as social media uses #hashtags to filter content. You might have categories for #school, #work and #soccer stories. Someone else might have #diving, #painting and #coding stories. Your story database contains both your own lived experiences and those you've heard about or experienced through others.

Any time you run into a situation where something unexpected happens (a Story Specs trigger), your narrative intelligence kicks into action. "Brain, we have a problem." Your NI starts to analyze the situation and wonders, "Have I run into a problem like this before?" To answer this query, it runs a search through your memory database for experiences like this one. In particular, it looks for a similar kind of problem—a similar pattern. If it finds a match, your brain then retrieves the experience and extrapolates the resolution for you to use to tackle your problem.

If it doesn't find a pattern match, it sends you off on a quest to figure out how to resolve this new kind of problem. Once you complete your quest and generate a resolution, your brain will file everything away in your database as a new story package.[3] Sound familiar? This is the Story Specs in action!

This problem-seeking, pattern-matching, resolution-making ability is what makes narrative intelligence so cool. It's a built-in expert system for solving real-world problems with solutions from real, lived experience.

Here's a simple example of how this works. Let's say you're on a canoe trip in the Pacific Northwest and you need to start a campfire in the rain. When you encounter this problem, your brain will try to find a story in your experience database in which you managed to do this previously. If it finds one, your brain recalls the information on what to do. You start the fire and resolve the problem. Anything new you learn during this specific instance of starting a fire in the rain is added to your existing database archive on #campfiresintherain.

Now, if your brain can't find a category for #campfiresintherain stories in your database, it sets off a bit of an alert that shouts, "New problem!" Then it starts to search for a story pattern that contains a problem as close as possible to the one you're facing.

As the brain explores your database looking for pattern matches, it will extrapolate bits of knowledge from stories in other categories that have similar—and different—patterns. Maybe you've never started a fire in the rain, but in high school you watched a friend set a bag of cheesepuffs on fire. Because this is archived in your database as a #fire story, your NI retrieves it and brings it to your attention. "Hmm," you think. "I happen to have cheesepuffs in my backpack right now. I wonder if I could use them to start my campfire?"

Boom! This is exactly how narrative intelligence fuels innovation.

Your brain uses patterns to search your story database for data—or intel—from related and diverse #categories that might help you resolve your new problem. Then it analyzes that intel to create insights about those alternate experiences. Your NI uses those new insights to generate new ideas, which you use to design a new way to start a campfire in the rain. Once you finally succeed and light your campfire with the cheesepuffs, your brain archives this new experience and problem resolution in your database under a new category of #campfiresintherain.

Narrative intelligence and innovation

So, your NI constantly does two key things that drive the innovation cycle.

One, it *deconstructs* and analyzes your archived experiences as stories to make sense of and learn from them. This story research and analysis process generates intel, insights and ideas that inform and inspire innovation.

Two, it *constructs* and designs future stories about how you might resolve a problem by sorting through the intel and insights to generate new ideas. As you progress through a problem-solving quest, you're constantly thinking, "What if I do this?" and "What if I do that?" For each "What if?" your brain creates a quick little imaginary test run as a future story to try the idea out to see what will happen. Though this story design (or creation) process typically occurs subconsciously, you'll discover in Part Two how to bring it to the surface and work with it as a powerful and intuitive way to innovate.

The narrative intelligence research

You can start to see why I find NI so fascinating, with such amazing potential to drive innovation. Now, can I prove any of this? Not yet. Science is just beginning to explore this field. To date, most narrative research has focused on what happens when we consume or deconstruct a story. No one has yet looked at how we can use it as a generative process for design and innovation. That said, there is some evidence to support my theories about NI.

To start, science has confirmed that we all have it. It is an innate human cognitive function. Our brains are physically wired for story. Research by neuro-economist Dr. Paul J. Zak and others has shown that stories generate measurable chemical and neurological responses, which trigger curiosity, enable analysis, fuel creativity, stimulate emotion and mobilize memory.[4]

Learning theorists from Jerome Bruner and Jean Piaget to Daniel Berlyne and Roger Schank acknowledge the cognitive sense-making function of narrative. This kind of intelligence is what enables us to fill in the blanks in a movie we're watching or a story we're reading. To be able to guess what's going to happen next. That's why we get impatient when a story teller goes on and on and on with "unnecessary" details. It's also what enables us to imagine alternate outcomes and different endings with the simple words *What if?* In fact, our NI capacity is so strong that it can create a sort of internal virtual reality system that enables us to get mentally and physically lost in a story. To lose track of time and space. Of our other senses.

This deep immersion is called a state of flow, a condition first researched and defined by Czech psychiatrist Mihaly Csikszentmihalyi in the 1990s. Triggering and sustaining flow is the ultimate goal of any game, movie, book or experience—and the sign of a great story designer. Csikszentmihalyi has written several books on flow—they're definitely worth a read.[5]

As the science of NI shifts and grows almost daily, this book can't be your definitive guide to NI research. If you want to know more, I suggest you start by exploring the work of the authors noted in the sidebar below, who work in this field and provide a good foundation of concepts and evidence that will help you leverage NI in a practical way.

NARRATIVE INTELLIGENCE RESEARCH SAMPLER

Kendall Haven

Story Proof: The Science Behind the Startling Power of Story is the book I've been wanting someone to write for years—comprehensive, credible and accessible. Though author Kendall Haven focuses on research that supports the use of story *telling* for education, he also shares many key research findings that have significance for story design and innovation. I've summarized my top three insights from his work below. (References to support these conclusions can be found in his book.)[6]

1. As mentioned earlier, our brain is biologically wired to process information in story. As we age and process more stories, the "wiring" gets stronger. This research finding corroborates anecdotal evidence that we make sense of, analyze, remember and share information that's presented in a story structure better than information offered via nonstory formats. We do indeed have a story-based, sense-making kind of narrative intelligence.

2. Research indicates that early exposure to and use of story structure for information processing leads to better math and logic skills later in life. So, the more we work through story, the better

we get at asking good questions, analyzing complexity and challenging assumptions—that is, thinking critically. As a side note, I'd argue that critical thinking is one of the most essential skills needed for innovation. It's also a skill most sorely lacking in the world.

3. We process information through the lens of personal experience. We make meaning from stories according to what we already know—information and skills stored in our own personal story database. This enables us to use our narrative intelligence to extrapolate and intuit the meaning and relevance of information, even if we can only access bits and pieces of it. Using a story framework, like the Story Specs, for design and innovation makes it possible for us to leverage experience and expertise we already have to close gaps and find solutions to complex problems, rather than starting from scratch. (Think #campfiresintherain.)

Paul Zak

Dr. Paul Zak has published some fascinating and rigorous research with compelling evidence. Zak is a master at making and sharing key scientific breakthroughs that help us understand how and why we communicate. His work shows how the brain and body react to dramatic conflict and demonstrates that stories that stimulate engagement and emotion can actually trigger changes to behavior, such as giving money. He also does a brilliant job of illustrating why we need to use stories in business and what value they generate.

Here are excerpts from a couple of his most popular articles:

"Why Your Brain Loves Good Storytelling": "We discovered that, in order to motivate a desire to help others, a story must first sustain attention—a scarce resource in the brain—by developing tension during the narrative. If the story is able to create that tension then it is likely that attentive viewers/listeners will come to share the emotions of the characters in it, and after it ends, likely to continue mimicking the feelings and behaviors of those characters."[7]

"Why Inspiring Stories Make Us React: The Neuroscience of Narrative": "Not only were we able to track what the brain is doing millisecond by millisecond during a story, we used the neurologic data to build a predictive model of donations to a childhood cancer charity—our measure of story impact. The statistical model we built predicts whether a participant would donate money with 82 percent accuracy. That is, by measuring how your peripheral nervous system responds to a story, we can almost perfectly predict what you'll do before you do it."[8]

Michael Mateas and Phoebe Sengers

This research duo published one of the first academic papers I read when I started my graduate investigation into narrative intelligence a decade ago—an insightful piece that continues to inform my work today. Their work speaks to the complex, interdisciplinary nature of NI as a foundational human trait. It also links NI to seminal cognitive and learning theory research done by academic narrative giants like Jerome Bruner and Roger Schank.

Narrative Intelligence: "By telling stories we make sense of the world, we order its events and find meaning in them by assimilating them to more-or-less familiar narratives. It is this human ability to organize experience into narrative form that David Blair and Tom Meyer call 'narrative intelligence' (Blair and Meyer 1997) and around which AI [artificial intelligence] research into narrative coalesces."[9]

Narrative intelligence as a superpower

As you start to become more aware of your NI in action, you'll realize that you're using it all the time, in all kinds of situations. And you'll discover that, when you use story as a cognitive framework, you're able to:

- analyze experiences,
- make sense of unfamiliar situations,
- define problems,
- identify potential resolutions,
- imagine future outcomes,
- package and archive experiences in memory as stories,
- sort stories according to meaningful categories,
- run pattern-matching searches through memory,
- retrieve relevant stories and
- share stories in a compelling way with others.

Unconsciously. Automatically. In nanoseconds.

Can you start to see why I call narrative intelligence our latent superpower? Latent because, for most of human history, we've focused on how we can use it to *tell* stories that educate, empower and engage audiences. However, I believe that we've just begun to tap its real potential. That we can find new ways to harness NI to change the way we design, innovate and lead. To simulate, create, test and share experiences that fuel creativity and learning. To generate better solutions for a better future.

Now, to do that, we need one more thing.

Design
A Recipe for
Innovation

W E NEED A RECIPE. The pros know that innovation takes more than a big idea, more than a fancy lab, more than angel investors. They know that, despite what you see in the movies, innovation is not some random, lucky process of staying up all night, working in your parents' basement, finally shouting "A-ha!" one day. It doesn't matter how deep your commitment runs or even how deep your pockets are, innovation doesn't just happen. If you want to innovate on purpose—if you want to be able to control, scale and repeat your innovation success—then you need a process. A recipe that tells you how to combine all your superpowers and secret ingredients to cook up a whopper of a breakthrough invention.

Design gives you that process.

Isn't *design* just another buzzword? Yes—and no. Because here's the thing. Design is another one of those really useful concepts that has been around forever, quietly practiced by geniuses from da Vinci to Jobs, who used it to radically reinvent our world. Repeatedly. Unfortunately, it popped onto the radar of management gurus about a decade ago and they proceeded to hype it so badly that it's now unrecognizable—somewhat like an overinflated balloon animal. In this section of the book, I'll try to cut through that hype, to show you what design is, how it works and how you can use it right now to start to innovate like a pro.

Defining design

You've probably heard the phrase *design thinking* at some point in the past few years. This isn't that. I still don't really know what the heck that's even supposed to mean. Forget that phrase. For our work, we're going to use *design* in two different ways—as a verb and as a noun.

As a *verb*, design is simply the act of solving a specific problem. Designers identify an unmet need (a problem) and they create an appropriate solution. The problem can be anything from an employee needing something to sit on to society needing to increase voter participation in elections.

As a *noun*, design is the outcome of the design (verb) process. It's the "thing" that designers create during the design process. The design noun of the design process to create something for your employee to sit on might be a chair. The design outcome of creating increased voter participation for society might be an online voting system.

DESIGN THE VERB

So, what do these definitions mean for us? The problem with today's innovation culture is that the world is only ever interested in *design* the noun. It doesn't matter if you work in tech or soup. Whenever we talk about innovation, people only want to know about the thing you're inventing: your new nanny-bot or cancer-crushing chowder.

No one wants to talk about *design* the verb. No one celebrates the design process. That's because they don't understand that you can't have one without the other. Think about the difference between story design and story telling. You can't tell a story until someone designs it. You can't make a movie until the writer goes through a story design process to produce a script. Right? You can't have the noun without the verb. So, if you're working in tech or soup innovation, you also can't whip up a new idea—an invention—without first going through the design process. Great stories don't just happen. Neither does innovation.

This brings us to one of the major barriers to innovation. You really want to do it. But you just don't know how. Few people can clearly describe exactly how to "do" innovation, how to design inventions, how to work through a creative process step by step. No one seems to have a recipe you can follow. Which makes innovation tricky to replicate, to do on command.

Now, this is where things get cool. Though you might not know how to design an innovative product or service, you do know how to design a story—thanks to your narrative intelligence.

What if you could combine your narrative intelligence with a framework like the Story Specs and use them to design something other than a story? What if you could follow a story design process to resolve a real-world nonfiction problem? To create something like an experience, strategy, product or service? Something that is different and new? Could you use story design as an innovation process? A problem-solving recipe? One that you could replicate effectively, efficiently, creatively, on demand?

Yes.

Story design for innovation

When you start to work as a story designer, you're going to make a major shift in perspective from being a user or consumer to being a maker, a creator.

Instead of looking at the Story Specs from the viewpoint of an audience member, you're going to go behind the scenes and put yourself in the story designer's seat. You're going to sit in the cockpit of a powerful story machine, with all kinds of controls at your fingertips— things like characters, resources, places and time. And you're going to design a story that describes the way a hero solves a specific problem.

Even though you can use the same overall process to design a real-world innovation project and a fictional story, there are a few differences to note between the two. For example, let's say you're going to design a fictional story about a hero whose best friend is paralyzed and can't walk. Your hero needs to invent something to help her friend get around easily. As the story designer of this story, you have to do all the work—all the thinking for the hero. You essentially design her quest to solve that problem. While you sit in the story designer's seat, you use all your controls—your story design joystick—to manipulate and make decisions about every aspect of the story. You get to define the problem, orchestrate the quest and choose the resolution. And you have all the time in the world to plan things out. The whole process can seem easy-breezy because you control everything. Maybe the hero invents a new kind of wheelchair—or solar-powered skateboard—or even a jet pack for her friend. Then they all live happily ever after.

This is what it means to be a story designer. A powerful creative. A problem-solver. It's insanely euphoric. Brilliant. Rewarding. Addictive. Because you are in total control.

However, when you sit in the design cockpit to start a real, live innovation project, you'd better buckle up and jam your helmet on tight, because you're in for one hell of a ride.

What's the difference?

When you're designing a story, you're one step removed from the process. You're designing a quest for somebody else—for a hero who is not you. You're able to see things from every angle, analyzing them before making any decisions.

When you're designing for innovation, you are both the hero and the designer. You're designing your own hero's quest in real time, as you work.

That's why innovation is so difficult. As the hero/designer, you are living the story every second. Instead of sitting at a nice, safe desk, coming up with big ideas and imagining how they might work, you're bringing them to life. Design for innovation is doing, not planning. Getting out into the messy world, trying stuff out and failing—a lot. You're making decisions live, on the fly, often when all hell is breaking loose, without knowing how things will turn out. That's why designers need a process to guide them. When you're innovating, you need a familiar, go-to way to make decisions about what to do next—how to solve problems in the heat of the battle.

That's where story design comes in. You already know how to do it. How to use your narrative intelligence to seek out and create solutions to complex challenges. In a pinch, you can easily fire up your imagination, pretend you are the superhero of a story and come up with some brilliant way to get out of a tough jam. Story design is the perfect "go-to" problem-solving process.

How do I know? Because I did this work, every day, for more than twenty years. This kind of live, on-the-fly story design is exactly what documentary filmmakers do. They make sense of complexity in ever-changing environments. They find ways to define the problem, design solutions and stay on mission. Design the story, get the shot, tell the truth and change the world. All in the moment. All on a shoestring budget.

My simple story design process helps you fire up your existing problem-solving expertise and start to use it as a step-by-step, methodical guide to navigate the complexities of a live innovation project. To tap your natural creativity and narrative intelligence. To work like a pro, to design anything you can dream of.

So, strap on your helmet, buckle up and let's go.

The story design process

You already know that every story describes a hero's quest to resolve a complex problem. That's the big-picture design process. In this section, we're going to break that down into actionable steps. Then, we'll try it out in Part Two.

First, let's start with the secret to great design.

If you only take one thing away from this book, this must be it.

The secret to great design is problem definition.

Say it with me. As a hero/designer, you have to know what the problem is before you can figure out how to resolve it. Makes sense, right? If you start to create a solution before you define your problem, your solution probably won't work. For example, if you ask an architect to design a building for you, she'll need to know what you want to use the building for, so that she can make sure her design meets your needs. Designing a home for a family of five is different from designing a soup factory. What would happen if she started to build a soup factory without determining your needs first, then found out halfway through construction that what you really needed was a home for your family? That sounds like a ridiculous example. Yet, we do this in the real world all the time.

We know from the evolution of the software industry that spending time early in a project to clearly define the problem saves big bucks in fixing bugs later on.[1] Still, this is a lesson society fails to acknowledge and apply in our everyday lives. When we encounter a trigger, we automatically assume that we know what the underlying problem is and immediately leap to the most obvious resolution. We don't take the time to pull back the curtain and put our narrative intelligence to work to make sense of the situation. To ask questions. Analyze what we know. Flag the things we don't know. Seek answers. These are all reasonable research and inquiry activities. So why don't we do them?

Our ego gets in the way. We get attached to our obvious resolution and resist letting go of it. And if someone challenges us, our first reaction is to dig in. Defend our idea. Take it personally. Why? Because we hate admitting that we don't know something. That we're not the smartest monkey in the room. That we don't have all the answers. We'd rather pretend we're on top of the situation and charge ahead with our big idea—even after we realize that it isn't going to work. That it's a waste of time and money. That we're solving the wrong problem.

Wasting time and money solving the wrong problem. Sound familiar? How many times have you seen organizations charge ahead with expensive initiatives that they know will fail, because they are too proud to admit that they might not really know what's wrong? Even if they do realize they're on the wrong track at some point during the quest, they rarely stop and cycle back to define the problem clearly. Why? Because assumptions are easy. Problem definition—not so much.

The secret to design for innovation is being able to admit that you don't know what the problem is. And that you don't have the solution—yet. The secret to design for innovation is being able to put aside your ego and activate your narrative intelligence to make sense of the challenge. To cut through all the complexity and chaos of a crisis and zero in on the root cause. Then—and only then—can you put on your hero helmet and start to design a solution.

Like I said, this is tough stuff. I think it's the reason we find it so hard to generate real innovation. Because it takes discipline to stay focused on problem and purpose. Not to make assumptions and leap ahead. Not to fall in love with a beautiful resolution that doesn't solve your ugly problem. Not to take it personally when your big idea flops big-time.

In my experience, getting the problem right is the single most important part of the design process. And I'm not the only one who thinks so.

> "If I had an hour to solve a problem and my life depended on the solution, I would spend the first 55 minutes determining the proper question to ask, for once I know the proper question, I could solve the problem in less than five minutes."
> —ALBERT EINSTEIN

Check out the following real-world examples to see what a difference problem definition makes.

Consultants like to tell the story of Audi's preparations to enter the twenty-four-hour Le Mans car race several years ago. The purpose of the competition was to win the race. Most teams assumed that building the fastest car possible was the best way to win. So, they defined that as their design problem and set off on their quests.

Not Audi's chief engineer. He took the time to analyze the complete challenge and realized that there could be several ways to win—several potential resolutions. To find the best one, he'd have to force his design team to be ultra-creative. So, he added a constraint and challenged them with this alternate design problem: "How can we win the Le Mans if our car is not the fastest?" Their response was to design the most fuel-efficient car possible. Reframing the problem to move past the obvious solution helped Team Audi realize that, by making fewer pit stops over the duration of the twenty-four-hour race, they'd be the fastest team overall. And they were right. Their innovative approach enabled them to win the race four years in a row.

Appreciative Inquiry (AI) practitioners often share this story to illustrate the importance of problem definition. Several years ago, an international airline struggled with high rates of lost luggage. So it hired an AI consultant to help it bring the numbers down. One of the unique features of AI is that it helps organizations create change by focusing on what's working well (opportunities) instead of what is broken (problems). As the story goes, when the management team explained the situation to the consultant, he said, "Let me get this straight. It's okay for you to lose luggage. You just don't want to lose as much of it?" "No—that's not right!" the team responded, somewhat exasperated. The consultant then worked with them to reframe their problem. In the end, they determined that what they really wanted to do was to design an excellent customer arrival experience—which included not losing customers' luggage.

Got it? Problem definition matters.

Now that you know the secret to great design, getting started is as easy as one, two, three. (Okay, four.) Like this.

THE 4DS OF STORY DESIGN.

When you look at the Story Specs, you see that the story quest—which represents the hero's design process—actually consists of many individual dots—or story beats—connected together. Each beat represents some discrete activity in the story—usually an attempt by the hero to resolve the problem. Remember, the dots in the quest can represent a multicentury narrative (like the history of space travel), a TV series with multiple episodes (like *Coronation Street*), or a ten-second story (like a gold-medal track sprint).

No matter how big the story is, if you zoom in to one specific beat, you'll discover that it actually works like a mini-story within the story—a bit like Russian stacking dolls. Each separate story beat has its own mini problem-solving or design cycle, with four specific steps: define, dream, dare and discover.

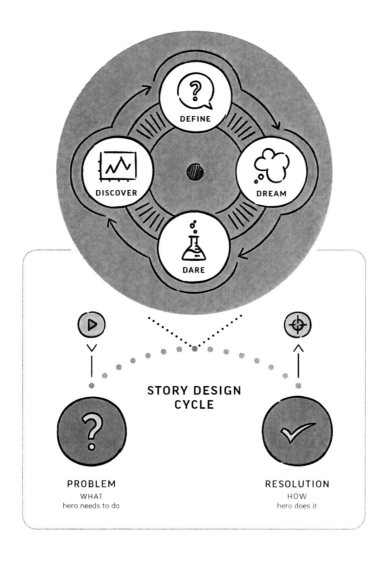

Let's take a look at the 4D story design cycle diagram above and expand on it.

DEFINE (Now what?)
Hero uses insights to (re)define the *problem*.

DREAM (What if?)
Hero imagines resolutions and generates an *idea*.

DARE (What happens?)
Hero tries idea and observes what happens to produce *intel*.

DISCOVER (So what?)
Hero analyzes intel to develop *insights*.

We know that in every story the hero has to solve a problem. And in most stories she (almost) never solves the problem right away because it's too tricky. Just like most of your real-world problems, right? Instead, she has to break down the main story problem into a bunch of mini-problems that she solves one at a time. For example, in *The Lord of the Rings*, Frodo needs to save the world from the evil Sauron. That's a big, tough problem to solve! At the beginning of the epic series, he has no idea how to do that. However, he does know that one of the first things he needs to do is to get to the nearby village of Bree to find help. So, the first problem he tackles is finding a way to get to Bree safely. If you know the story, you know that doesn't go so well! He gets attacked by the bad guys and almost dies. Then, when he gets to Bree and thinks he has succeeded, he discovers that the wizard who was supposed to meet him there to help him has disappeared. So, now, instead of a resolution, he has a new problem. What to do next?

If you map this all out with the 4Ds, you can see that, as a story hero tackles each mini-problem in her quest, she actually works through a complete problem-solving design cycle. She defines the mini-problem, dreams up a potential resolution, dares to try her idea out and fails or partially succeeds. She then processes what she learned from that experience to discover what she should do next, moving on to the next dot—the next piece of the problem—to repeat the cycle.

Throughout her quest, the hero/designer repeats this cycle over and over again, moving from dot to dot in the Story Specs to develop, test, reject, select and refine potential resolutions to her problem. Along the way, the initial story problem may shift and evolve, forcing the hero to react by altering her design choices during her quest.

The cool thing about this quest structure is that you can expand and contract it to work with your own real-world problem at any scale. You can focus on one specific moment in time or the narrative of the past ten years, for example.

The story of how James Dyson invented his cyclone vacuum brilliantly illustrates the iterative nature of the quest design cycle. It's reported that he spent five years building, testing and rejecting 5,126 different versions of his invention before he got it right.[2] If you mapped his innovation quest onto the Story Specs, you could tell the whole story in just a few beats by choosing some highlights. Or you could zoom into every one of his iterations to see how he worked through the four steps 5,127 times to define, dream, dare and discover the ultimate resolution.

Story design for engagement

Looking at Dyson's quest this way also helps you start to see how you can use this story structure to design engaging stories for communication and story-telling work. As the designer of a story quest, you can control how many beats a story has and what happens in each one. You can set up a series of multiple problems for your hero to resolve, forcing her through multiple versions of the 4D cycle. As she struggles with one problem after another, each one riskier and more difficult than the last, your audience gets caught up in the story. Their narrative intelligence kicks into action and they start to problem-solve in their heads along with the hero. "What will she do next?" they wonder. "If I were her, I'd—," they think.

Forget everything else you've learned about story telling. This, right here, is the secret to engagement. Learning to use the story design cycle to set up problems for your hero and create dramatic tension—to manipulate the story "gap"—is the only surefire way to get and keep your audience's attention. The great story designers are masters at this—drawing us into our hero's evolving problems over hours, months, years—and many sequels. As long as the hero has an unresolved problem that the audience members care about, they will stay engaged.

To end your story, you need to structure the design quest so that the hero runs out of options. She must get to the point where she has done everything possible to resolve her overarching problem—to save the world from evil—and has only one idea left to try. It is her most desperate play. The thing she was hoping to avoid. Now, with time running out and no choice, she must risk it all to solve her problem—or die trying. At this stage in the story, your audience will be on the edge of their seats, waiting to see what happens. "Will she make it? I can't stand the suspense!"

The instant the audience finds out what happens, their engagement ends. This is the other secret to great story design. Once the hero comes to the end of her quest and there are no more problems to resolve, the story is over. It doesn't really matter how things turned out for the hero. The quest is complete and the audience disconnects mentally, emotionally. This is the end. Forget the long wind down. The dénouement. Today's audience has no patience for lengthy conclusions. Stop writing and call it a wrap.

Design challenges

When you sum the whole "design as problem-solving concept" up, it all seems pretty straightforward, on paper at least. Which leads me to ask again: Why is our society so terrible at innovation?

Design is scary. As a creative process, innovation is inherently ambiguous because we don't know what the outcome will be. And that's terrifying for a lot of people. Most folks get very uncomfortable when you ask them to take on a project that will lead them into unknown territory. That involves going on a quest that doesn't have a predictable ending. As a society, we don't like risk. Uncertainty. Or change. So, fear becomes a big barrier to innovation. That means you need to find ways to manage that fear if you want to create breakthrough change. Because it doesn't matter what you're designing—things rarely go as planned. You start every project with a brilliant idea, a seemingly obvious solution to your problem. Yet, your initial ideas will rarely work right out of the box. Every design project has lots of twists and turns—just like a great story. That's why you need a reliable design process—to give your teams a familiar, easy-to-use roadmap to guide them through the scary swamps of innovation.

Design is crazy hard work. As I mentioned, real-life innovation doesn't happen like it does in the movies. You don't just "have a knack" for design, for creating those things. Wave your wand. Press a button and make it so. It doesn't matter what you're designing—a story, a strategy or even a service. Great design is a lot of work to do it well. It requires patience and perseverance. Commitment to the process. Great design is exhilarating. Engaging. And exhausting. It's also the difference between solving a problem just to check a box and creating something of value that generates real impact. Adequate versus amazing. This is why great stories are so rare. Because we all might have narrative intelligence, but designing compelling, memorable, meaningful stories is a ton of work—even for pros like me!

This is also why we have so little great innovation and so much crappy design in our world. Most people don't do the work. They take shortcuts and produce crappy stuff. Crappy strategies, services and products. Crappy stories. Crappy all-around innovation. A good design process makes it easier to stay on track, do the work and get great, noncrappy innovation.

Design is user-focused. We humans are predominantly self-focused. Most of us think that everyone else in the world is just like us. That means that we also think we know everything about them. So we don't bother to leave the safety of our (office) cocoons to go out into the messy real world and learn about other people's problems. That's a waste of time, right? Because we already know—or assume we know—what our users need. And we know that our idea is so brilliant, everyone will love it. Even if it doesn't meet a real need or solve a real problem. We think that users should adapt to and adopt our ideas—we shouldn't have to adapt our ideas to their needs.

But great designers and story heroes are not like that. They are authentically user-driven. People-driven. Frodo doesn't do what's best for him—he does what's best for the world. He throws his comfortable life away and risks everything to destroy the ring, to make life safe for his people. Obama, Gandhi, Mother Teresa, Elon Musk, the Dalai Lama—pick your favorite hero and take a closer look at his or her approach. They are all designers—innovators—trying to invent a better future. And they do it by getting out into the real world, to meet the people they serve and try to define their problems.

This is the basic concept behind the entire field of human-centered design. It's also the driver for the emerging field of behavioral economics. Designing for innovation requires us, as design heroes, to get past our assumptions and get to know the people we're designing for. Do that and I guarantee you'll discover a whole new world of problems (and opportunities) for future innovation.

Design is deliberate. By definition, *design* the verb means making decisions and doing things *on purpose*, with the intention of resolving the problem. Compare this with the way we do a lot of other things in life—thoughtlessly, carelessly, unintentionally. Without thinking about the consequences or impact of our actions.

When you practice design for innovation, every single thing you do is deliberate—no matter what you're creating. There is no auto-compile. No shortcut. You never get to coast. Cruise. Cheat. As the designer/hero leading a quest, you're constantly reflecting and analyzing. Thinking about what the real problem is, what purpose you're trying to achieve and what to do next. Each step is a conscious decision, informed by previous steps, by doing the work.

Sticking to a defined process, a methodology like this requires discipline. You have to stay focused on achieving your goal. Everything you do contributes to your purpose. If something doesn't advance your quest or move you closer to a resolution, you don't do it. You skip it. Ditch it.

The same is true in story design. Hollywood calls this "killing your darlings." Creatives like writers and filmmakers know that every single thing in a story must contribute to moving the story forward. Otherwise, it gets cut. With our amazing narrative intelligence, we can fill in the blanks for almost any story instantly. So, don't bore us with your extraneous details! Keep your story design clean and lean.

The beauty of making everything so intentional is that you know that all your efforts are contributing to solving the problem. They have value. You are not distracted or spinning your wheels. Not only does this mean that you design better solutions, it also means you don't waste precious resources trying to solve the wrong problem. Which brings us to the main reason we stink at design.

Design is problem-focused. We are not. We are solution-focused. We'd much rather chase dreams of glory and soar with the stars than spend time peeling back the layers of the situation, trying to discover what's at the core of our challenge. What the real problem is that we need to resolve. So, we charge ahead with our big ideas and ignore everything else. Because it's easier to rationalize the pursuit of a solution that sounds brilliant than it is to activate our narrative intelligence, ask hard questions, challenge assumptions and invest time in making sense of the real problem at hand. In my experience, this solution bias is the biggest barrier to great design, to breakthrough innovation.

In other words, the theory is logical and predictable. The people who put it to work are not. That's why we need practice. That's why we need Part Two.

IN PART TWO, I'll introduce you to some of my favorite tools and techniques that can help you manage all these challenges. You'll fire up your narrative intelligence to start working like a designer to turn your big ideas into breakthrough innovation. With the Story Specs as a guide, you'll discover how you can use story design to solve real-world problems and design (almost) anything.

Part Two
How to Do Story Design

The Tools and Techniques You Need to Succeed

WELCOME TO PART TWO! Ready to get your hands dirty?

It's time to shift from thinking about story design to doing it. Taking action is the foundation of innovation—getting out of your head and into the real world to develop, test and refine ideas.

Trouble is, there are few practical tools and techniques to guide you through this work. That's why I developed the Story Canvas. In my strategic work, I discovered a need for an agile, intuitive design framework that anyone could use to study, shape and share solutions to (almost) any kind of problem.

In Part One, you got the theory. You discovered the Story Specs—a deceptively powerful story model that helped you learn what narrative intelligence is, how it works and how you can use it for innovation and engagement. You also explored design as a problem-solving process—getting a feel for how it works and why you should use it, what value it adds.

Part Two gives you easy-to-use techniques to help you put all this theory into practice and start problem-solving like a designer.

First, you'll explore the Story Canvas, a creative multitool you can use throughout your design process. You'll take a tour of the Canvas to see how it works and how it connects to the Story Specs.

Then, you'll work through step-by-step guides on how to use the Canvas for research and design. As you work, you'll discover how to activate your untapped narrative superpowers to find and use fresh intel, insights and ideas to advance your project. By the end of the book, you'll have everything you need to start using story design as an agile, accessible and affordable platform for innovation.

Story Canvas™
A Creative
Multitool

AT A BASIC, functional level, you can use the Story Canvas in two ways. You can use it to *construct* and *deconstruct* stories. Create things and break them apart. In design language, this means you can use the Canvas for research (deconstruction) and design (construction).

As a side note, as we go forward, I'll often refer to the "thing" we're designing as a "story." Just remember that the story design process works for all kinds of other things too. In your mind, feel free to substitute your own innovation—like a strategy, experience or service.

Now, I know that both *research* and *design* have a million different meanings to people. At a high level, here's how I use them.

Research describes any activity that produces useful intel to inform the decisions you make during your design process. Most people do research at the front end of an innovation project, then never do any more. This approach guarantees failure. As you saw in Part One, research is embedded in the 4D story design cycle. Designers ask questions constantly and need to do research throughout their quests to inform and improve their ideas. One of the easiest and most powerful ways to do this kind of design research is to use the Story

QUEST

PROBLEM
What does the Hero
need to do?
What Problem must
s/he Resolve?
If–

DEFINE
NOW WHAT?

Hero uses Insights to
(re)define the Problem.

DREAM
WHAT IF?

Hero imagines
Resolutions and
generates an Idea.

PURPOSE
Why does this
story matter?
How will it change
the world?
–then

DARE
WHAT HAPPENS?

Hero tries Idea and
observes what happens
to produce Intel.

DISCOVER
SO WHAT?

Hero analyzes Intel
to develop Insights.

INTEL
What facts are critical
to the Quest?

INSIGHTS
What does the Hero
learn during the Quest?

What actions does the Hero take to resolve the problem?

What specific challenges arise?

How does s/he overcome them?

RESOLUTION
What happens
at the end?

What does success
look like?

IDEAS
What opportunities
emerge during the Quest?

Canvas to collect and analyze (or deconstruct) stories. Through this kind of story-based research ("story research" for short), you can produce rich qualitative intel, design insights and original ideas to inform and inspire innovation.

Design (the verb) typically describes everything the hero does during the quest that's focused on creating a resolution to the design problem. Using the 4Ds of story design as a reference, this includes activities to define emerging mini-problems, dream up ideas, dare to test them and discover useful insights. As the hero/designer, you can use the Story Canvas to plan, organize, track, assess and share each step in your design process.

Though they may not sound sexy or glamorous, research and design are the foundation of any innovation process. By spending time now to learn the basics of both and practice with the Canvas, you'll be ready to activate your narrative intelligence any time you need it.

My guess is that you'll need the Canvas right from Day One—because one of the toughest things about leading any kind of innovation project is getting started. All my work in the past few years has been with leaders who came to me because they needed to do something new and different—and didn't know where or how to begin.

That's another reason why I created the Story Canvas. You don't need some fancy, virtual reality, intergalactic app to kick-start your innovation work. You simply need an easy-to-use, tangible worksheet that you can share with collaborators. A place to dump all the stuff that's in your head. To help you organize, sort and make sense of what happened in the past, what's happening now and what you need to do in the future. A tool that steers you in the right direction and gets you working like a designer.

At first glance, you'll note that the Story Canvas resembles the Business Model Canvas (BMC) created by Alexander Osterwalder and his colleagues.[1] They really pioneered the idea of creating agile tools to capture, share, prototype and refine ideas—tools that enable you to move from concept to action quickly—instead of investing heavily in creating massive tomes like business plans that go into great detail and become obsolete before they're even finished. Today, multiple kinds of canvases exist for various business functions. The Toolkit Project[2] and Blank Canvas[3] offer online access to many of these—definitely worth a browse to see if any might be helpful in your work.

Though the Story Canvas was inspired by the BMC, it serves quite a different purpose. As a design worksheet, I set up the Story Canvas to act as both a roadmap and a dashboard; it includes all the key elements you need to plan, track and share your innovation project. The Canvas gives you a snapshot of your project status and next steps. And it works as a guide, helping you figure out what to do next.

We'll dive into the many ways you can use the Canvas and see how it works with a real-world example later in this chapter. First, let's zoom in for a quick tour of each of the elements.

Title

This is pretty self-explanatory. When coming up with project titles, I like to use snappy, unique descriptions that everyone on the team can remember and share. It also helps to make it fun and audacious—to stretch the limits of your imagination a bit. If you can't get creative and go a little crazy here, how will you ever cut loose enough to get to the frontiers of innovation?

Hero

Naming the hero of your story design project can be trickier than you think. In Chapter 3, you discovered two kinds of story design heroes: the hero/designer in a real-world innovation project and the lead character in a story. The former should be straightforward, as this is typically the person leading the venture. If you're launching a new project, put your name here.

If you're designing a story to share with others, you probably want to put someone else, like your customer, in the HERO box. Why? Take a look at this example.

Let's say I'm a company like Climate Smart that helps organizations reduce greenhouse gas (GHG) emissions and save money. And I need to design a story to share about how we helped Jane's Tires cut GHG emissions by 10 percent. In this situation, I would probably put the CEO Jane in the role of hero. Then, I could design the story to show how Jane resolved her emissions problem and became the hero of her company's energy future—with the support of me and my organization, Climate Smart.

Why would I make Jane the hero instead of me (and my company)? Why put myself in a lesser, supporting role? Wouldn't I seem more amazing as the hero?

That depends on what problem you're trying to resolve with this story. (Now you see why you need to define your problem first.) Why do you want to tell this story? Who is your target audience? What do you want to change? Why does this story matter; what's your purpose?

If your purpose is to help potential clients see how they can buy your services and become "climate heroes," then you want to create a hero (Jane) who is just like them. This might seem counterintuitive until you discover this little secret to great story telling: *No one wants to hear your story. Deep down, they don't really care about you.* Rather, we all want to see ourselves in your story. Remember, we are inherently egocentric, self-focused. We need to know why your story is relevant to us. What it means to us. Why we should care. This is our narrative intelligence at work again. If you tell me a story about Jane's Tires, and I can't see myself in it, I will not engage with it. I won't care. And you will fail to achieve your purpose, which is getting me to buy your services.

Make sense? Try it out next time someone starts to tell you a story. See if you can figure out who the hero is. Then reflect on your gut reaction to the story. What happens if/when you hear about a hero's experience you can relate to—when you see someone like you? That is the magic of story at work.

So take your best shot at naming your hero here. You can always change it later!

X-factor

You can use this box for a couple of things. I've included it to make you stop and be intentional about why you're starting your project. What is it that makes your problem, idea, story or project extraordinary? Why do you need to innovate? If you don't know this, you need to spend time figuring it out—for a few reasons.

The X-factor identifies the "thing" that makes the problem unique, original, challenging.

If you're designing a new strategy or service and you don't have an X-factor, then you're not innovating. More troubling, you probably also don't have a unique competitive advantage. That might be okay—though it's something you'll need to address when you get to the problem and purpose for your project. (Hint: If you already know the resolution to your problem, then you don't need innovation. Just do it!)

If you're designing a story to share, the X-factor is the thing that engages the audience—helps to trigger our curiosity. Remember that unresolved problems are the "hooks" that get and keep our attention. If you don't have an X-factor—if your story has a predictable resolution—it won't engage us. It also won't be memorable enough for our narrative intelligence to tag, store and retrieve it later.

For example, what's the X-factor for a flying car? A house-sharing service? A reusable rocket?

Though your X-factor might be obvious, it's worth recording here, as it will be one of the key design criteria that will guide you and help you make decisions during your innovation quest.

PROBLEM
WHAT
hero needs to do

Problem

By now, you should be a problem expert! In this box, you want to note your project design problem—or your story hero's problem—as clearly as possible. What unmet need are you trying to address? For whom?

Beware of the problem/resolution trap here. Remember the chair design problem we encountered in Chapter 3? The design problem was to find a way for the employee to sit comfortably at her desk. Not to design a new kind of chair. This problem has many potential resolutions, one of them being a new kind of chair. The problem should not be a resolution. Resist the urge to assume you know the answer to the problem here. The problem is a need that you don't yet know how to meet.

Purpose

Your purpose is the *yin* to your problem *yang*. It tells us why this project matters—how it will change the world. When you look at the Story Canvas, you'll see that problem and purpose are two halves of an *If—Then* statement. If you solve *x* problem, then you will generate *y* impact. You need to keep problem and purpose aligned throughout your work. I give a few tips in Chapter 5 for how to figure both of them out.

Quest

The quest is really the heart of any story design process—where all the action happens. As a key element of the Story Canvas, the quest provides structure and guidance for your design journey. When you're innovating, it also works like a real-time dashboard, offering a snapshot of what you've done, where you are and how far you have yet to go.

In Part One, you saw that you can deconstruct the quest of the Story Specs™ into a series of individual story beats. And that you can zoom in and out of your story quest as needed, to focus on one tiny specific beat or capture the entire history of a narrative. The Story Canvas mirrors this beat structure, allowing you to use it in the same way. When you look at it, you'll see that I've deconstructed the hero's quest on the Canvas even further, to reflect the 4D story design cycle you discovered in Chapter 3.

Each box in the quest represents one story beat. Each story beat includes four discrete steps that the hero must follow as she tries to design a resolution to her problem. The four steps form one complete, mini problem-solving or design cycle.

Let's expand again on the 4D story design cycle diagram.

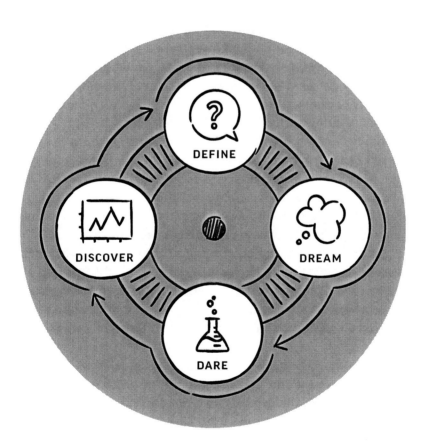

4D STORY DESIGN CYCLE

DEFINE (Now what?)
Hero uses insights to figure out what *problem* to tackle next.

DREAM (What if?)
Hero comes up with an *idea* that might resolve the problem.

DARE (What happens?)
Hero tries idea and observes what happens to produce *intel*.

DISCOVER (So what?)
Hero analyzes intel to develop *insights*.

Your hero works through this four-step process in an iterative way, step by step, beat by beat, until she reaches the end of the quest and finally resolves her problem, gives up or dies trying. As the story or innovation designer, your job is to figure out what the hero does at every single step and record it on the Canvas. When you're done, you'll have a complete story timeline that describes each decision the hero made during each of the story's mini-design cycles.

"Hmm," you're probably thinking. "Working through that level of detail looks way too onerous and complex." Don't panic. Once you start working with the Canvas on your first project, you'll realize that you actually do all four of these steps all the time. You work through this kind of mini problem-solving cycle in everything you do. Sometimes it's easy and automatic; other times it requires more focus.

Still, it looks like a lot of work, right? Why bother? What's the point of recording every step of your quest journey? Remember all the barriers to innovation we discovered in Part One? You can start to see now why I say that design can be crazy hard work. And—here's the payoff—the return on investment (ROI) for staying true to the process.

When you deliberately work through and capture each cycle, you can start to see patterns in the way your ideas and actions play out. Maybe you have a hidden bias for a certain kind of resolution. An aversion to others. Or unexpected brilliance on your team that you need to leverage. It's a bit like doing a complex math problem—if you don't make your work visible and give yourself time to reflect on it, it's hard to figure out where you went wrong and where you could do better next time.

Taking the time to articulate and track each step of the process also gives shape and meaning to your emerging innovation story so that you can share it with team members, stakeholders and funders. In one concise snapshot, they can see exactly where you are in the quest, what you've done, where you're going and why it matters. Having something tangible to share also makes it easy for them to activate their own narrative intelligence and pattern analysis to introduce new ideas and intel to the quest, based on their own experiences and story databases.

Don't worry if this all feels a bit overwhelming right now. We're going to spend time practicing each of the 4Ds later.

Intel

The bottom of the Canvas includes three "parking lots" for you to use throughout your project, starting with this one for Intel. When you dare to try out your best *what if* idea from each dream phase, you'll generate data about what happened. These data can come in many forms, including observations, measurements, reports and reflections. Limit your intel collection here to the facts only—things you know or saw. This is the *what happens* box. Maybe your great idea caused an explosion, crashed the server or made a customer cry. All these outcomes are data. Don't try to guess why things happened or what they mean—just record the facts. Note your key findings here for future use. And be sure to find a way to collect and manage all the data you produce during your project, as they'll provide you with valuable intel that can help you figure out what to do next.

Insights

After you finish testing your idea and complete the *dare* step, you'll move on to *discover*. This is where you analyze or make sense of the intel you just produced, to develop insights that will inform your next step. Specifically, you'll want to use these insights to help you define the next mini-problem you need to solve. This is the *so what* box. Use it to record your key insights from this analysis in the form of patterns, trends and themes. You can also use this space to capture other A-ha!s, deep thoughts, hunches and inspirations that emerge at any point in the story design process.

Ideas

Once you analyze your insights to define your next mini-problem, you iterate and start a new mini-design cycle. During the first step—*dream*—you and your team imagine a *what if* idea that might help you resolve your problem. "Hey, what if we ...?" While in this dream phase, you'll likely generate more ideas than you can use at the time. Don't toss the rest out—no matter how nutty or useless they seem at the time. You never know when you might need them. Instead, park them here, in the IDEAS box, as potential resolutions that you might want to test at some point.

Resolution

This is The End.

How you use this box will depend on your project. During an innovation project, you may get to a point in the quest where you've finally figured out what the final resolution should be. This usually happens after working through many iterations of the 4D design cycle. Once you get to this stage, it can be helpful to state or sketch that final resolution in this box. You still might have a few more steps to complete in the quest—like finding investors or the right partner to manufacture your solution. Having the resolution in plain view will give your team a clear target to focus on and help keep everyone on track. This is similar to the way many writers design stories. They already know how they want things to end. So they capture that resolution here—then reverse-engineer the quest (work backward) to ensure the hero makes it happen.

You could also use this box as a placeholder for several potential resolutions—then design the quest to test out their viability, feasibility and desirability (three common measures of any innovation).[4]

Most of the time, if you're using the Canvas to track your progress on a project, filling in the RESOLUTION box will be the last—and most satisfying—part of your design work. Recording the way that you finally resolved a wicked problem helps you shape your impact story, making it easy for you to share your experience and insights with funders and stakeholders.

My X-factor

WHAT MAKES THE STORY CANVAS SPECIAL?

Now that you've had a chance to explore the Story Canvas, you're likely starting to see that it is more than just a worksheet. It's a multiuse tool for your innovation venture. A flexible research and design platform that's structured specifically to help you leverage the untapped narrative intelligence you discovered in Chapter 2 and use it to lead the messy work of innovation. You can use the Canvas across your project, to guide big-picture development over a decade or to dive into the details of designing a tiny widget.

So, that sounds cool and all. But here's the thing. There are lots of other canvases and innovation tools out there. What makes the Story Canvas special? What is the X-factor?

In plain language, the Canvas gives you and your people *a simple shared approach to problem-solving*. Incredibly, this is something most of us lack. As I highlighted in Part One, we don't learn real-world problem-solving in a methodical way at school, at home or on the job. Even worse, decades of scientific and logic bias in decision-making theory and management practices have discredited the one natural problem-solving process we all do have: narrative intelligence.

I created the Story Canvas explicitly to meet this need. In design terms, the problem I resolved was filling a need for *a simple shared approach to problem-solving.* My purpose in designing the Canvas was to make it easier for you to innovate. And here we are, back to problem and purpose.

WHY DO PROBLEM AND PURPOSE (P&P) MATTER FOR INNOVATION?

Why am I so obsessed with P&P? Because you have to know your problem and your purpose before you can figure out the value proposition (VP) for your innovation. And you have to be able to articulate your VP if you ever want to sell your idea. You have to be able to help others see the value in your offering.

What is value? It's change. It's the difference in your user's life with—and without—your innovation. The difference between life with a problem and life after the problem is resolved.

For example, let's say that I have a problem: I need my dirty house to be clean and I don't want to clean it myself. (Yes, this is a real-world problem for me!) One potential resolution to this problem is for me to buy a housecleaning android to do the work. The android creates value for me—changes my life—by doing the work to transform my house from dirty to clean. Your purpose, as the inventor of the android, is to make it easy for me to have a clean house. So, the value proposition for your android is that it creates a clean house for me. As the hero/designer of the cleaning android, you have solved my problem and achieved your purpose. Your resolution has clear value to me.

Now, what would happen if you built an android that was an expert banjo player instead? What would be the value proposition for me? Nil. I don't have a problem that could be resolved by such an android.

As the hero/designer on an innovation project, your job is to generate a resolution that matters to the user—that has real value. That's the essence of innovation. To do that, you have to know what she needs and why her problem matters. You might also have to help her discover that she has a problem in the first place. Maybe a banjo-playing android would drive all the slugs out of my vegetable garden. Maybe it would help me sleep and I just don't know it.

This is where business strategy and marketing come in. Making users think they have a problem—from sleep deprivation to a slug-infested garden—is the first step in trying to sell them your product. I can't see value in your innovation until I know that it will solve a meaningful problem for me. That's why problem and purpose matter for innovation. If you can't make these two concepts clear, then you won't be able to articulate your value proposition either.

This all seems pretty straightforward. Yet, most innovators still struggle to articulate value. Why? A couple of reasons.

First, as we learned in Chapter 1, problem definition can be hard work. It's a lot easier to skip it and assume we know what the problem is. Sometimes we're right. More often, we're not—and we waste time and resources chasing solutions to the wrong problem. If your innovation doesn't solve a real problem, then it doesn't create value. At the time of this writing, a smart watch is cool, but most people don't *need* one. It doesn't solve a pressing problem for them. So they're not willing to spend hundreds of dollars to buy one.

Second, a lot of us simply don't want to admit that we just want to innovate for the sake of it. We secretly don't care if our "Big Idea" solves a real-world problem or not. We are in love with the idea of creating something new and different—and refuse to give it up—even if and when we discover that it has no value. Generates little or no ROI for the user. Remember the story design process of Hollywood writers I talked about, where they have to kill their darlings when they discover that they don't move the story forward?

The same applies to design and innovation. Great designers can admit when their ideas don't work. Don't create value. Don't solve problems. Why? Because they are driven by problems—not resolutions. Walking away from a brilliant idea isn't easy for them. Nor does it make them happy. But it does make them better designers. So, before you get started as an innovator, know what problem you are trying to resolve, who your user is and why it matters.

OTHER BENEFITS

You don't have to limit your value proposition to just one thing. For example, the VP for the Story Canvas goes beyond giving you a simple shared approach to problem-solving for innovation. You can also use the Canvas to:

- provide an innovation roadmap that guide the process and tracks progress,

- engage and align teams by making challenges and goals visible,

- enable iterative development and testing of big ideas,

- keep you focused on action and outcomes,

- support the use of non-narrative tools and processes in your quest and

- make it easy to share the emerging story of your innovation with others.

Cool, eh? All in a single page you can use on the train, in a board-room, on your phone or online. Now that you have a feel for the Canvas, let's see it in action.

5

Story
Research
An Insight
Generator

E
ARLIER, I WROTE that we can use the Story Canvas in two basic
ways for innovation and story projects—to *construct* and to
deconstruct stories. Up until now, we've focused on using story
for design as a framework to construct, produce, make, create something. It could be a service, a strategy, an experience, a product—even
a story. In fact, most of the world focuses on constructing and telling
stories as a way to lead, to influence. In particular, we seem obsessed
with finding ways to use story to report results, outcomes, solutions.
The End is all that seems to matter.

However, if you flash back to what we learned about narrative
intelligence in Chapter 2, you'll remember that we all have this innate
ability to deconstruct—unpack, analyze and make sense of—what
happens during the entire story, instantly, easily. Yet, we rarely use
this intelligence explicitly, methodically, as a way of exploring, learning
and studying what's happening during real and fictional experiences—
and why.

So, while the world focuses all its energy on constructing stories to tell, it is completely missing out on the flip side of NI. Because here's the thing.

As we learned in Part One, every single one of us has our own rich, unique database of stories in our memory. Tagged, sorted, processed. Each one of these stories is essentially a little package made up of a problem, quest and resolution. In other words, every single story in our memory is actually a prepackaged resolution to a specific problem. Think about it. In every single one of our stories, the hero has already figured out how to resolve the problem. And we have recorded her actions, the way she did it, in our memory of that specific story quest. We know what worked for her. And what didn't. Remember the #cheesepuffs #campfiresintherain story?

That means that every story package in our memory includes a roadmap (quest) that shows us how to resolve that story's specific problem. Every single archived story includes intel, insights and ideas about the entire problem-solving process—not just the resolution. (*Design* the verb, not just *design* the noun). And we can recall and use this quest intel anytime to help us figure out what to do when we encounter similar—or new—kinds of problems.

Reframed, that means that every single one of us has a unique story database of intel about how to resolve all kinds of problems. Every single one of us is actually a walking library of hidden design expertise.

That is freaking huge.

What if you could find a way to collect and analyze a group of these story databases to find out how the heroes resolved a specific kind of problem? What worked, what didn't and what would have worked better? What could you learn? What discoveries could you make? How could this fresh intel help you make sense of your own problems? Generate insights about hidden opportunities? Uncover ideas for radical new resolutions? Evaluate your own resolution for improvement and scaling?

The untapped potential of our collective narrative intelligence to fuel innovation is massive. There are more than 7.4 billion human libraries of lived experience on the planet right now, ready to help you design better futures.

Awesome. So. How can you access some of that fabulous stored intel for your project? Through story research.

Process

These days, research comes in many flavors, with confusing labels: qualitative, quantitative, design, market, behavioral and so on. Each flavor works in different ways, producing different kinds of data, which are analyzed in different ways to generate intel, insights and ideas. Innovators use different flavors throughout the design process to develop, test and scale their ideas.

Story-based research is my favorite flavor. For the academics in the crowd, my approach is based loosely on grounded theory.[1] Keen nonacademics might want to read Dr. Brené Brown's description of her research for a great explanation of how it works.[2]

One of the reasons I love story research is that it's a relatively straightforward inquiry that anyone can do with a bit of practice. Essentially, it offers a methodical way to use your narrative intelligence to collect and analyze one or more stories. To tap into the experiences and expertise that we just discovered are hidden in each of our story databases.

The story research process we're going to use has three main steps:

1. Define question(s).
2. Collect stories.
3. Analyze stories.

By working through these steps in a structured way, you can generate intel that describes what happened, insights about the implications of these observations and ideas that are inspired by your analysis.

Though this sounds like a lot of work, you actually do story research all the time, every day. Every time you encounter a new kind

STORY RESEARCH PROCESS

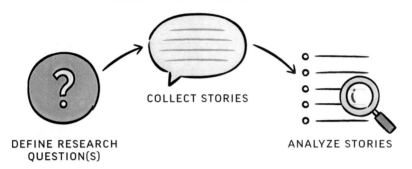

COLLECT STORIES

DEFINE RESEARCH
QUESTION(S)

ANALYZE STORIES

of challenge, every time you listen to a story in real life, you use your narrative intelligence to make sense of and define the problem. You also use your narrative intelligence to study the quest—the hero's actions—to see how she resolves it. When you do this during your daily activities, you do it in a way that is automatic, informal, unconscious, unplanned. You frame questions, collect stories and analyze responses in just nanoseconds.

Professional researchers use story research in a more structured way, to study complex subjects that range from addiction to marketing to education to economics. For example, Brené Brown's popular research on courage and vulnerability draws on her decades of story-based research. Global innovation leaders like IDEO use it for design research to help them identify and solve customer needs.

Why would giants like these use stories to inform their work instead of something like big data? After all, analytics based on big data collected from millions of people can tell us a lot about *what* users do. That's pretty cool. You know what's even cooler? Story research. Because it tells us *why* people do things. And if you're working on any kind of project that involves human behavior, understanding *why* people make specific decisions is essential to your success.

What's the difference between this kind of story research and narrative analysis? Not much, really. The latter tends to describe a more rigorous, academic approach to this kind of work. Remember the difference between story and narrative: Stories describe a specific experience in which a hero solved a problem. And narrative describes a collection of related stories or experiences, typically unfolding over time. In practice, narrative analysis and story research essentially use the same approach. The main difference shows up in your research question—in what you want to learn through your analysis. When you do a narrative analysis, you're trying to understand the meaning of multiple stories within a larger context. When you do a story analysis, you seek to identify specific lessons learned by the hero as she resolved a specific problem. In addition, narrative analyses tend to be in-depth investigations of an issue. A story analysis can be a deep dive as well—or it can focus on one specific story and take just ten minutes to complete (as you'll see soon). So, the differences between the two are subtle. And in the end, they really don't matter. You can call this kind of inquiry whatever you like! The bottom line is that you can use it to collect and analyze stories in a methodical way to discover all kinds of useful things.

For example, let's say you're a real estate developer who is trying to figure out where to launch your next big project—in an emerging, trendy zone downtown or the roomy suburbs? (This is a real-life example from one of my projects.) So, you ask some people to tell you stories about buying their most recent home. Your group includes two guys who are demographically identical in big-data language: same age group, income, education, background, ethnicity, family status, even job. One just bought a condo downtown; one just bought a house in the burbs. That's all the intel you're going to get from big data. But you need to know *why* they made two different choices. You need to come down from thirty thousand feet to ground level—to hear them describe their specific experiences and decision-making process. Once they both do that, then you can deconstruct and compare their stories, to see if you can find insights that help you understand not only the *what* and *how* of their home-buying story but also the *why*. As we just learned, *why* matters because it links directly to your purpose and your value proposition.

Sounds amazing, right? So why don't we do this more often? Because we have a bias for numbers. We've been taught to believe that they are more reliable, more accurate, more truthful than the kind of descriptive, open intel you get from stories. We like the black-and-white numbers we get from research tools like surveys, polls and online tracking systems. We also like the fact that these kinds of tools are fast, cheap and easy to use. Yet, one of life's great truths is that you get what you pay for. Professional researchers know that data gathered through these tools can be notoriously inaccurate at identifying people's true values, beliefs and needs. "Check the box" kinds of research limit the ability of respondents to share values, beliefs and experiences freely. Instead, we know that people who take surveys tend to respond with the answers they think researchers want or expect.[3]

However, when people tell us stories, they reveal hidden knowledge, values and desires in the telling—ideas and thoughts they don't even know they have. These are grounded in reality—in their personal experiences—which makes them tangible and actionable. *The intel generated by story research goes much deeper than tracking online clicks and likes—it reveals the secrets of human behavior.* That's the true value of story as a research tool. The main reason people don't use story for research is simply that they don't know how. That's why we're here.

The next section includes practical tips on how you can combine your narrative intelligence and the Story Canvas to do your own story research in a methodical, deliberate manner, just like the pros. Through this work, you can make sense of the problems you need to tackle as a hero/designer—and discover unexpected insights that trigger breakthrough resolutions.

Just a reminder, though, this is a how-to book for innovation—not a guide to qualitative research. If you'd like to learn more about this field, check out John Creswell's book *Qualitative Inquiry and Research Design: Choosing Among Five Approaches*.[4] It's also worth noting that the techniques I use are deliberately quick and easy. If you need in-depth, bulletproof research to inform something like the design of a government policy or a lifesaving medical device, story research can give you a good start—but you'll need to combine it with other, complementary methods.

So. Let's start at the beginning.

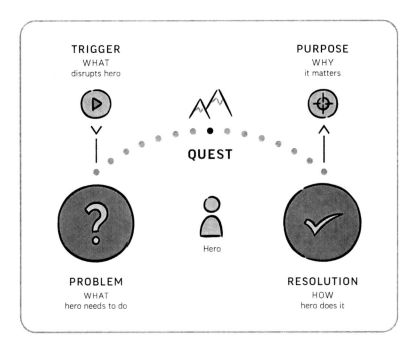

Uses

The first thing you need to know is that story research projects are actually design projects that follow the Story Specs approach. Luckily, you now have a pretty good idea of how that works! Each project has a research question or problem that you as the hero/designer need to resolve. Each project follows a quest for answers. And each one generates intel, insights or ideas as a resolution. An entire story research process might unfold in just a split second in your brain—or take a lifetime to complete.

One of the things I love about story research is that you can use it at any point in your project to help you get the information you need to figure out your next steps. I tend to use story research for three main things:

1. Before the project starts, to help *define the design problem.*
2. During the project quest, to *generate useful intel* that supports decision-making.
3. After the project resolution, to *assess the impact* and effectiveness of the end result.

Here's how story research works for each one.

1. DEFINE THE PROBLEM.

Gah. Yes. Here we are. Again. Problem definition.

Remember: The first thing you need to do at the start of every design or innovation project is to define the problem you need to resolve. Because the nature of your problem will dictate the approach you take to resolve it.

That sounds easy in theory. But as you learned earlier, when you kick off your big new innovation project, you might already know what problem you (as the hero) need to resolve—or you might not have a clue. Often, the problem space is so big and complex—or wicked—that you find yourself overwhelmed, unable to zero in on one specific problem to solve because they all seem intertwined.

Story research is the fastest and easiest way to get started when you're stuck at the beginning of a project like this. It's a powerful tool that helps you make sense of—deconstruct and distill—all kinds of complex situations. And focus in on something specific. That's because every time you use your narrative intelligence to analyze a story, you automatically break it down into its individual parts (like the dots in the Story Specs™) so you can figure out what problem the hero is resolving.

By using structured story research at the beginning of your project to help you make sense of your big hairy problem, you can zoom in on and define one specific real-world challenge that you want to tackle quickly (and cheaply). Remember how we used the Story Specs to soar up to thirty thousand feet to describe abstract narratives, then back down to ground level to share one very specific story beat? This does the same thing.

For example, right now I'm working on a big public-sector innovation project with a broad purpose: to help students make post-secondary online learning even better. The X-factor for this project is that my client wants to focus on figuring out what role students can play in designing resolutions. This is new, as the education system historically has focused on the abilities of faculty, institutions and ven-dors to innovate—not students. As you can see, the initial purpose is quite general—a messy wicked problem with all kinds of complexity and components. In fact, like many innovation projects, it is made up of multiple, integrated problems that can't easily be untangled. So, the only practical way for my client to get started was to find one specific tangible problem to tackle within the giant wicked space.

To do that, I helped them do story research at the beginning of the project. As part of a larger event, called the sxd (Student Experience Design) Studio, twenty-five students came together from multiple cities, towns and disciplines to share stories. Specifically, I had them work in groups of three with this assignment: *Tell your group about a specific excellent online learning experience you've had. It could be about some-thing you did at school—or at any time in your life. Maybe you were learning a language, doing a home repair or learning a new game. Make sure your story is specific, tangible and personal.*

Once they finished sharing stories in their groups, the group mem-bers analyzed their stories to identify key themes or desired elements of excellence. Things that made those stories memorable and great. (You'll learn how to do this in the next section). To do this, they had to ask "Why?"—a lot!

Why was that an excellent learning experience?
Why did you choose to learn that way?
Why did this help you learn?
Why—?

Through this analysis, the groups came up with ten things—ten elements of excellence in online learning. These represented things that they wanted more of—things that they could use as a starting point for innovation. For example, one of the elements of excellence was truly interactive content. Once they identified this, they could then use it as a design problem:

> How might we empower students to generate interactive content to make online learning even better?

Very quickly they went from having no idea about where to start to having a specific problem they could realistically tackle. One problem that is part of the bigger problem. This is the secret to problem definition: figuring out what you want and why you want change, then reframing it as a problem to resolve.

You can see, on page 88, how this project looks on the Story Canvas.

2. GENERATE INTEL.

Though the example above focuses on using story research for problem definition, it also offers some clues about how you might be able to use the same process to uncover bits of information and insight that spark *new ideas* for innovation. In that example, the students not only defined the problem but also identified nine other insights they could use as springboards to new ideas that would make online learning even better. Using story research to generate intel can be quick and easy.

For example, I worked with a not-for-profit organization based in a resort town that wanted to find ways to grow the local economy. Almost everyone and every business in the town was dependent on the "mother" corporation that ran the main resort, and on tourist dollars. My client's theory of change was that if they could strengthen the local economy, then the town would become more sustainable—and more resilient in the face of possible declines in tourism or changes by the "mother" corporation. In this case, they had already defined their problem. However, they weren't sure how to get started. They wanted to find intel they could use to seed innovation and to engage local entrepreneurs in the initiative.

So I designed and led a "story storm" research event for local entrepreneurs. (A story storm is like a brainstorm, using story as a way to trigger ideas.) Specifically, in pairs they shared and analyzed stories about personal experiences they'd had creating change. I chose this because I wanted them to identify unique strengths they'd already used successfully to do something new. (This is an engagement design trick. It's easier to take on new challenges if you build on something you've already done well in the past.) In just two hours, twelve entrepreneurs identified several characteristics unique to their village, including an affinity for rational risk-taking, powerful vision, commitment to community and, interestingly, a preference for working collaboratively.

Figuring out how to use this intel in the quest then became the next problem they had to resolve. After our session, my client worked with the twelve entrepreneurs and used this intel to develop an action-based opportunity to strengthen the local economy and facilitate the creation of shared value. From this simple story research, they ultimately launched their own local economy action network (LEAN) to foster homegrown business ventures.

You can see, on page 90, how this project looks on the Story Canvas.

DOING STORY RESEARCH is straightforward in this situation, where you have a relatively familiar problem to resolve. But how do you collect stories to inform innovation when you're trying to create something totally new—unlike anything anyone has ever experienced? About a topic that doesn't exist? The best way is to ask questions about related or similar experiences. Or sometimes about wildly different experiences you think might be linked. For example, if you're working on something related to space tourism, you might ask about adventure travel. Or bungee jumping. Or scuba diving. Can you see how each of those topics relates to space tourism? Once you collect and analyze those related stories, you'll find it easy to extrapolate your findings to your crazy new big idea. You'll see an example of how this works in the next section.

TITLE SXD	**HERO** eCampusOntario

QUEST

PROBLEM

If we can help students make online learning in Ontario even better—

PURPOSE

—then we can increase learning outcomes and student success.

DEFINE
NOW WHAT?

How might we figure out a way to tackle this giant problem?

How might we use the 10 elements of excellence to help students lead innovation in online learning?

DREAM
WHAT IF?

What if—we ask Denise to design and lead a one-day SXD (Student Experience Design) studio to explore opportunities for student-led innovation?

What if—we create imaginary scenarios of online learning experiences based on one or more of those elements of excellence?

DARE
WHAT HAPPENS?

25 students attend SXD studio. First activity is for them to share experiences of excellent online learning in groups of 3.

Students work in teams to sketch stories of future learning experiences based on elements.

DISCOVER
SO WHAT?

Students analyze experiences and identify 10 things that made those experiences excellent.

Students identify 7 realistic opportunities for ways they could innovate.

INTEL

- 25 students attend.
- Students share 25 stories in French and English.
- Participating student ages from 16 to 58.
- Several students from virtual high school also attend.

INSIGHTS

STORY CANVAS™

How might we develop those opportunities to share with potential supporters?

RESOLUTION

Story research unpacks the "big" problem into 7 specific mini-problems that the student teams can work to resolve.

• Students identify 10 key elements of excellent online learning, including clear and concise content, resource-rich, useful and pleasing, and adaptive.

IDEAS

Students generate 7 ideas for learning innovation, including:

• Virtual reality (VR) welcome kit
• Student-generated VR content in courses
• Real-time simulation coaching
• Artificial intelligence as learning concierge

| **TITLE** | **HERO** |
| Story storm to generate intel | Centre for Sustainability |

QUEST

PROBLEM
If we can strengthen the local economy—

DEFINE
NOW WHAT?

How might we take the lead to strengthen our local economy?

How might we engage local entrepreneurs in generating intel to start to resolve this problem?

DREAM
WHAT IF?

What if—we bring local entrepreneurs together to try to solve this problem?

Ask Denise to design and lead an event for local entrepreneurs.

PURPOSE
—then our town will become more sustainable—and more resilient to possible declines in tourism or changes by the "mother" corporation.

DARE
WHAT HAPPENS?

Consult with community partners to gauge interest.

Denise leads story storm. Entrepreneurs share stories in pairs, about personal experiences they'd had creating change.

DISCOVER
SO WHAT?

Great response to idea—should go ahead.

Entrepreneurs analyze stories. Discover many unique key skills and traits.

INTEL

- 12 entrepreneurs participated.
- Group analyzed stories to identify over 120 strengths and assets of the local economy and community.
- Synthesized these into 20 key traits.

INSIGHTS

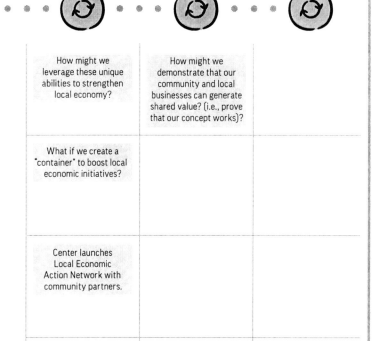

			RESOLUTION
How might we leverage these unique abilities to strengthen local economy?	How might we demonstrate that our community and local businesses can generate shared value? (i.e., prove that our concept works)?		Ongoing, homegrown LEAN initiative with local businesses supporting local businesses.
What if we create a "container" to boost local economic initiatives?			
Center launches Local Economic Action Network with community partners.			
Community very receptive—tremendous interest in concept of shared value from local businesses.			

Top traits:
- Vision
- Relationships
- Collaboration
- Inclusivity
- Strong entrepreneurial culture already has required independence and leadership for community change

IDEAS

- Establish a shared value, community co-op for residents, in which members collaborate actively to develop and strengthen independent, local, shared value enterprises.
- Run *Dragons' Den* style events to choose local businesses.

3. EVALUATE RESOLUTIONS.

You can also use story research to evaluate and assess completed inno-vation projects. This is actually the easiest and most straightforward application of this research method. You basically collect and analyze stories that describe people's past experiences with your "thing" to find out what worked well and how it could be even better. This is a tremendously powerful way to find out why customers buy your product, donate to your charity or decide not to join your fitness group.

For example, I had a client who had been running a community garden project for several years. The client's purpose, however, was not to help people grow their own food. Rather, he wanted to use the garden as a way to help people in the community build connections—specifically with adults who have developmental disabilities. When he contacted me, he had a hunch that the program wasn't working.

So I ran a story research project to evaluate the program. I inter-viewed six people who had been members of different gardens for different amounts of time and collected stories of their gardening experiences. This included finding out why they had joined the gar-den (what problems they wanted to resolve), what happened during their experiences (what they did to resolve their problems) and what outcomes they had (what resolutions they designed).

Then I analyzed the stories to look for patterns (which you'll learn to do in the next section). I quickly found a disconnect between my client's purpose and the purposes of the six people. They all joined the garden primarily to grow food. Developing relationships was secondary.

So there was a misalignment or gap between the gardeners' needs and my client's resolution. This is a classic case of deciding on a reso-lution before defining the problem—something that could have been resolved if the client had done story research before he started.

You can see, on page 94, a quick sketch of that project on the Can-vas. Pretty straightforward, right?

THIS IS THE MOST common kind of evaluation that people do. It's called a summative evaluation because it comes at the end of a program or initiative. Recently, I've also been doing a lot of work that uses story research to assess, guide and improve innovation projects as they evolve. This kind of ongoing assessment is called developmental evaluation (DE). Rather than waiting until something is finished to assess how well it works, DE helps innovation teams evaluate their ideas iteratively, almost in real time, throughout the process of creating, testing and refining their innovation.[5] By using the Story Canvas as a framework, you can use DE to help improve your work, engage your team and track your development journey so that you have a ready-to-share story for funders and stakeholders.

To do this, you essentially become an observer of the ongoing design process. As the developmental evaluator, you track, document and help the team reflect on each story design cycle in order to learn what's working well and how to do things even better.

Method

Now that you know the three main ways to use story for research, let's get into the specifics of designing and running a story research project using the Story Canvas to see how you can make this work for you.

At a basic level, story research mirrors the scientific method you learned in school. You come up with a research question—an idea you want to test or something you want to learn about. (In other words, a hypothesis, hunch or theory of change.) You collect some data about your idea. Then you analyze and make sense of the data to see what you can learn about your hunch.

In our story research process, you take the same steps.

1. **Define your research question(s).** What do you need to learn? What problem are you solving? What idea do you want to test?

2. **Collect your stories.** Go on a quest to find and record descriptions of people's real experiences and expertise (data) related to the problem.

3. **Analyze your stories.** Sort, deconstruct and find patterns in story data to produce intel, insights and ideas that resolve your question.

| **TITLE**
Community Garden Evaluation | **HERO**
Community group |

QUEST

PROBLEM

If we establish a community gardening program that's accessible to adults with developmental disabilities—

DEFINE
NOW WHAT?

How might we help adults with developmental disabilities develop meaningful relationships in their communities?	How might we evaluate the program to see if it is providing the desired benefit?

DREAM
WHAT IF?

What if—we start a community garden program?	What if—we use story research to analyze the experience of gardeners in the program?

PURPOSE

—then those adults will increase the number and quality of relationships they have in their community.

DARE
WHAT HAPPENS?

Get funding and launch 40 gardens.	Hire Denise to conduct story research. Collect stories that describe the experiences of 6 gardeners.

DISCOVER
SO WHAT?

Participants don't seem to develop new relationships	Analyze stories for patterns. Discover people join gardens to grow food—relationships are secondary. Takes 3 years to create connections.

INTEL

- 1,700 participants.
- Most interviewees grew up in families that grew/celebrated food.
- All interviewees experienced theft of food from gardens.

INSIGHTS

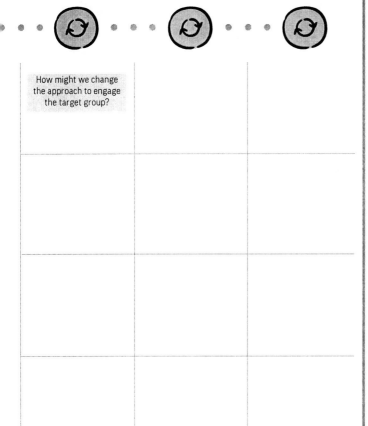

How might we change the approach to engage the target group?

RESOLUTION

- Narrative evaluation summarizes intel, insights, ideas.
- Suggests story design problem for future work:

  How might we move beyond providing simple and fleeting connections—to create conditions in which people can engage in developing lasting relationships through making 3- to 4-year investments in pursuing a shared goal?

- Interviewees rarely saw other people when they were at the gardens.
- People join primarily to garden.
- Few members of target group participate in gardening on their own.

IDEAS

- Organize more events.
- Pair target group with community participants.
- Track ongoing stories and experiences for real-time learning.
- Try new organizational structure for better engagement.

STORY RESEARCH PROCESS

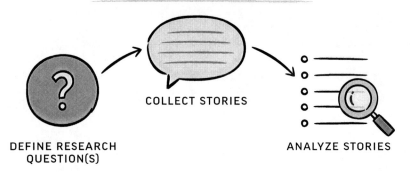

COLLECT STORIES

DEFINE RESEARCH
QUESTION(S)

ANALYZE STORIES

You can use the Story Canvas to frame and guide your story research project no matter what you're researching or where you are in your innovation quest. So grab your Canvas and let's start at the beginning.

1. DEFINE YOUR RESEARCH QUESTION(S).

In most story research projects, you play the role of hero/designer. Again, just like all hero/designers, you need to start the project by figuring out what problem you need to resolve, what question(s) you need to answer.

Why start here? Because this is still a design project, which means that you need to define the correct problem or question to help you choose the best story collection and analysis tools for your research quest. Fortunately, defining the question in story research tends to be pretty straightforward. That's because most story research is triggered by real, specific problems in an existing project or venture. It's driven by a need or a gap in knowledge that has already been identified.

For example, if you're developing a new online grocery story, you need to know about the way people currently buy groceries—or what they like best about online shopping. So, defining the research question(s) should be easy-ish. Once you have it, you can add it to the Canvas in the PROBLEM box. Don't forget to add your title, hero and X-factor to the Canvas too.

2. COLLECT STORIES.

Once you've defined your research question(s), you need to go on a quest to collect stories you can analyze to look for intel. Kind of like collecting tissue samples to study a disease. Or forensic evidence at a crime scene.

Before we get into the details of how to do that, we need to spend a minute looking at the difference between the way your subconscious narrative intelligence handles collecting and analyzing stories in your day-to-day life and the way we do it in a story-based research project. Why? Because a planned research project treats story collection and story analysis as two separate activities, while your everyday narrative intelligence automatically intertwines the two. Like this:

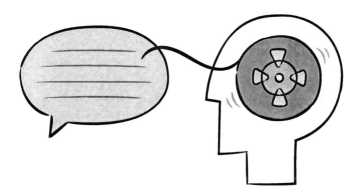

As soon as we encounter a story—whether it's in a book, on TV or at the lunch table—our narrative intelligence kicks into action. A story recorder in our brain turns on to start writing the story into our memory (i.e., collect it), while our pattern finders begin to deconstruct it (i.e., analyze it), looking for clues that help us define the problem. Some folks, like journalists, have really strong NI and are experts at managing the dual tasks of collecting and analyzing stories simultaneously. However, if your goal is to collect stories as part of a research project to generate ideas and intel, it's usually best to design an approach that enables you to collect and record the stories first, then take time to study them later. Otherwise, you risk missing the best intel.

If you haven't done this kind of work before, this approach might seem like overkill. After all, on the surface, collecting stories sounds dead easy. You simply ask someone to tell you a story about x. Or you throw up a call to action on your website that shouts, "Tell us your story!" and let people have at it. Right?

Not so fast. The thing about story collection is that the stories and data you get will only be as good—and as precise—as the questions you ask to trigger the stories. It's that pesky problem definition thing again. If you ask someone to share a story and don't give them any parameters or guidance, you might get something wildly insightful—or you might get something totally useless. This leads us to the three secrets to good story collection:

1. Design great trigger questions.
2. Create inviting experiences.
3. Produce useful story records.

Although these sound obvious, it's easy to mess them up through lack of planning. So let's look at how you can design your methods to get them right.

SECRET 1: Design great trigger questions.

When you start to think about what questions to ask people to trigger stories for your collection, you have to make sure your question(s) links back to your overall research question or hypothesis. This is along the same lines as making sure that the problem you're trying to solve in your design project aligns with your purpose.

For example, when food trucks first became a trend, I had a client who wanted to get in on the action and start his own food truck business. First, though, he needed intel. He needed to know what his customers would want. How to create value for them. Which of the many problems they had would be most important for him to resolve with his food truck.

Now, if food trucks had been around for a while when he was starting his business, and people had lots of experience with them, then he could have simply collected customer stories of excellent food truck experiences and figured out what he needed to do. In this case, the trigger question would have been something like: *Tell me about a time when you had an amazing meal at a food truck. Why was it amazing? What specific things happened? How did they make you feel?*

However, at the time, the industry was so new that few people had ever eaten at a food truck. So they didn't have personal experiences to share. Why not just ask clients directly what they would want in a food truck? That might generate some insights. But most of us are unaware of our subconscious needs, of what drives our behavior, decisions, choices. We couldn't answer that question even if we wanted to. Instead, as the hero research designer on my client's innovation project, I had to figure out a way to surface the hidden desires and values of his potential customers. When you need to research a topic that is new or even nonexistent, you have to get creative. You have to find a way to bridge the current reality of your research subjects and the potential future of your innovation. The easiest way to do that— to identify tiny nuggets of intel—is to get people to tell you stories about a relevant/similar experience. Make it easy for them to make the leap between *what is* and *what could be.* For this project, I used this trigger question: "Tell me about the best takeout dining experience you've ever had."

Takeout food would be the closest real-life experience they could have. As the participants in our story research described their experiences, they unconsciously included details and clues about their food influences. Then, while I listened to the stories, I was able to flag these nuggets and focus in on them to learn more, asking these follow-up questions, leading them from their actual experience to a desired, imagined experience:

What made it the best takeout meal?
What was most memorable?
What would have made it even better?

What would your dream takeout experience be?
Why would you like that?

Through this process, I was able to identify tiny glimmers of insight that sparked an unexpected innovation opportunity—an educational food truck for diabetics.

Designing research questions like these can be tricky. You want to make sure you give people enough guidance to trigger stories that are useful, on topic. At the same time, you need to stay open and objective so that you don't bias their responses. It's also important here to frame your questions so that people tell you about their experience— not just what they ate. (The entire problem, quest and resolution. Not just The End). As always, you're trying to understand what problem they were trying to resolve by eating a meal. That may sound silly, but the choices we make when we eat are driven by multiple needs that go beyond consuming food to survive. Why were they eating that specific meal, in that specific place, at that specific time, with those specific people? What choices did they make during their quest for food? What did they enjoy the most? What would they do differently?

When collecting stories, you also need to help people remember and unpack their experience quests step by step, story beat by story beat. Your goal is to gather enough information about the experience to enable you to retell the story accurately on your own—complete with problem, quest and resolution. Note that all the questions listed above ask people to tell me about a specific experience—not about what they tend to eat in general. Remember that stories make big-picture and abstract concepts concrete, tangible. Asking for specific stories instead of descriptions about usual practices generates the kind of detailed data you need to make sense of a problem—and produce jackpot-level intel.

Designing great questions is more art than science. And it takes practice. It helps if you rehearse or test out the questions in advance. Try them out in your head or on colleagues to see what kind of answers you get. The best story research questions are structured enough to help someone focus on a specific experience and open enough to give her room to surprise you.

Now, how can you work with the Story Canvas here? Use it to test out your questions. Note the question in the PROBLEM box. And the reason you need this intel in the PURPOSE box. Then ask a helper to respond to your questions and record her answers in the QUEST section of the Canvas. Did you get all the information you need? What is still missing? What new or different questions would you need to ask to be able to record, retell and analyze the story accurately?

Now that you have a good start on your story collection questions, how do you go out and get the stories you need to answer them?

SECRET 2: Create inviting experiences.

Cultivating the optimal user experience for story collection is another critical part of designing your story research method. This kind of experience design is something most people never think to do until they discover that one tiny bad experience can instantly kill their entire project. Believe me—I learned the hard way during my decades of documentary filmmaking.

To get this right, you need to anticipate every single barrier that could prevent someone from sharing their (sometimes very personal) emotions, experiences and expertise. Sharing stories is an intense process during which we often reveal hidden thoughts and ideas. This can make us feel extremely vulnerable, afraid, nervous. Your job, as the hero/designer, is to take the time to design a story collection experience that explicitly mitigates all those scary feelings and makes it easy for me, as a story teller, to open up with you. Depending on your project, you might also have to find ways to make story sharing social, fun or rewarding. In short, you have to ensure there are zero barriers that could discourage people from participating.

You'll typically find yourself working with two different story collection methods: face-to-face and technology-mediated. The first is obvious. The second can be anything from paper-based journals to video conferences to online web forms. Each method has its pros and cons. Choosing which to use is one of the many story research design decisions you'll have to make.

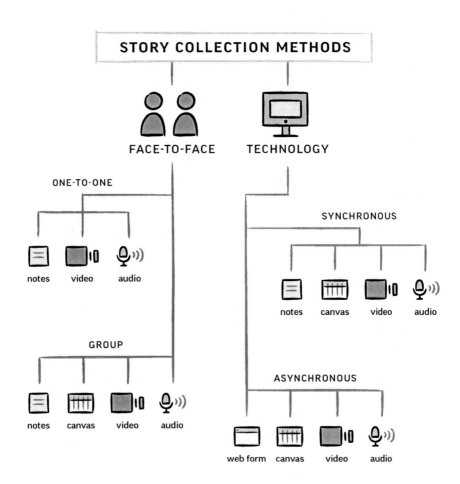

STORY COLLECTION: FACE-TO-FACE

Given a choice, I will always collect stories using a face-to-face method. My preference is to do one-on-one interviews.

That said, I also love collecting and simultaneously analyzing stories in groups. My experience has been that group story shares are one of the most powerful ways to inform and inspire innovations.

What's the difference, and how would you choose?

One-on-one interviews enable you to interact freely with the person sharing the story. This is helpful because it gives you the opportunity to build a bond before getting into any tough questions. (Sometimes a tough question can bring an abrupt end to an interview!) This approach also gives you space to ask clarifying questions as the interview unfolds. If you need to go deep into a story, to dig for details, this is the format to choose. This is what I did for the community garden project.

Collecting stories in a group can work in a few different ways.

- You can set up something like a circle and invite individuals to tell you stories about a specific experience. You'd record all those stories, then take them away to analyze later. This way, you'd get to collect stories from everyone in the group.

- You can do the same thing as above, except you ask the group to analyze the stories they hear on the spot. You might have ten people share ten stories—and have those same ten people analyze the stories. This is what we did for our resort-based economy project and the food truck project. More about how to do this in a bit.

- You can get people to share stories with each other about the topic in pairs or small groups. Then you might ask them to summarize insights or retell the best story from their small groups to you and the entire group. This is a great way to engage and learn from large groups. The downside is that you only get the highlights that group members select to share; you don't get to hear or collect stories from everyone in the group. This is how we did our story research for the online learning project.

- An alternative group approach is to ask everyone to record the stories in their pairs/small groups and give you the recordings for later analysis. A version of this is to send out "recorders" to do this across a workplace or community. This way, you get to collect stories from everyone. However, you wouldn't hear the stories firsthand, nor would you have control over the quality of the recordings.

Obviously, you'd choose your approach based on your research question and design problem. If your focus is to find new intel, ideas and insights hidden in the stories, then you'd choose a method that would enable you to access and analyze all the stories firsthand. If, however, your main problem is to engage others in your innovation project, I'd recommend using the group approach. We'll look at this more closely in the next section on analyzing stories.

Okay. Let's say you decide to use a face-to-face collection method. How can you design the best experience for this work?

Essentially, you need to think about creating a cocoon. You want to completely shut out the outside world. Eliminate all barriers and distractions. Turn off phones. Close doors and blinds. Power-down computers. Pull chairs close together. Move tables and desks out of the way so there are no physical barriers between you and the person(s) telling the stories. Create a world that is just you and the story teller(s), safely isolated from everything else. This is true for both one-on-one and group story collection.

That's the physical space. Designing a safe emotional space can be trickier, especially if you're working in groups. You need to do a little role-play work here and stand in the shoes of your story teller(s). Consider who will be in the room. Who will be sharing and listening to the stories? Will there be power differentials? For example, a boss and an employee—or a funder and a grant-seeker? What's the nature of the stories you're collecting? Would I feel embarrassed or afraid to tell my story in front of a group? Who are the story tellers? Are they comfortable speaking in front of groups? Will they be sharing stories in their first language? These questions and others become your design criteria for your story collection—helping you make decisions about how to create a safe, encouraging and effective experience.

STORY COLLECTION: VIA TECHNOLOGY

Though I'm considered to be a bit of a tech expert in my work, I'm also the first to recommend against using any kind of technology in story collection. Simply put, anything that gets between you and the person sharing the story creates a barrier to engagement. Period. I don't care if it's a pencil and notebook, or holographic VR recording studio. Naked, raw human connection is the best way to go. Unfortunately, it's also the most resource-intensive. Sometimes, we have to compromise.

Typically, you'll find yourself using technology in one of two ways. In a live, real-time kind of experience, which is called synchronous. Or a delayed, not-real-time, asynchronous setting.

Synchronous story collection includes live, real-time activities like video and audio recording, note-taking, sketching and live-journaling. These activities almost always include some way to capture the stories in a digital or analog format (aka electronic or paper-based media). Activities like video recording often require a team of people to operate all the equipment, particularly if you're capturing a keynote presentation.

When designing this kind of story collection, you need to keep the following in mind:

- Make sure the technology works seamlessly. Any malfunctions will distract the story teller and lower the quality of data you collect.

- Minimize the number of support people in the room. It's intimidating to tell your story with a huge video crew or gaggle of managers looking on. Kick out everyone who doesn't absolutely need to be there.

- Do your homework. Rehearse the process. Be ready and anticipate potential problems. Technology breaks down. All the time. Have backup cameras, microphones, batteries ready to go. Have a contingency plan for when the system collapses. Because it will. Do everything you can to protect your story teller from the anxiety and chaos linked to technology operations. All you want her to think about is her story. Everything else will become a distraction that worsens the experience.

- If possible, have someone else manage the technology so that you can focus on creating your bond, your cocoon with the story teller.

- Make sure that you can hear and understand the story teller. Otherwise, the whole thing is a waste of everyone's time.

Asynchronous story collection, which doesn't happen in real time, can be a bit more forgiving. However, this approach is also less effective simply because you're not there to guide it. The upside is that this approach always includes some form of recording. So you're ensured of generating some data (though not necessarily the best data).

This approach usually requires you to prepare a series of story questions that anticipates the story tellers' responses and ensures that you cover all your bases. The risk here is that you'll miss a clue that indicates the teller has rich experience to share about a specific part of the story. In addition, this approach includes the same challenges addressed above, in that technology always creates a barrier to engagement.

On the plus side, designing this kind of story collection can be a bit easier, as you can test and refine your collection tool before launching it. In addition to designing questions that help you make sense of the story, you'll also want to consider your analysis method. How will you organize and work with the stories you collect? Will you use a spreadsheet? Sticky notes? Audio files? Stories can be long and complex. Planning ahead to manage the data you collect will help guide your collection method. I'll share tips about this in the section on story analysis.

You can use the Story Canvas here as an outline to guide the design of your story collection tools. All the main questions are already listed in the boxes. Using them as a foundation, you can create paper or online forms, surveys, spreadsheets or even storyboards with step-by-step questions for people to answer. This approach works to help you collect and record stories in any format—paper, online text, video, audio, even drawing and photography.

The next section includes a few ideas on how to capture and record stories.

SECRET 3: Produce useful story records.

The main reason you collect research stories is to analyze them to generate intel, insights and ideas. That means you need to design a useful way to record the stories. Taking notes or relying on memory might work for one five-minute story. But capturing and managing hundreds of long stories for a big project requires a rigorous process and planning.

My rule of thumb for story collection is to record everything—unless I can't—simply because it makes my analysis work more valuable and more accurate. Being able to take time to sort, analyze, make sense of, review, compare and reflect on stories after collecting them always enables me to generate additional ideas and insights. Think about what happens when you watch a movie or read a book the second time. You always notice details that escaped you initially.

That said, raw stories shared as data can be long, windy, messy and filled with irrelevant content. Your recording design process will have to take this into consideration. How and where will you record the stories? How big will the digital files be? How many stories will you collect? Who needs to access them? Where and how will they access them? Will you need to transcribe them? Do you have to keep the recordings secure? Are you subject to privacy and/or ethics regulations?

You might find it useful to create a checklist to make sure you've addressed all the key design considerations, to help you develop your recording plan.

Let's go back to our two story collection methods to see how recording could work.

STORY RECORDING: FACE-TO-FACE

In qualitative research, story recording is often called "primary data collection": getting story data in the first person directly from the source. Though you have many options for face-to-face story record-ing, the most common is audio recording, because it's cheap, easy and less intimidating than video recording. You can use any kind of device you like to do this: computer, digital recorder, smartphone and so on.

Just make sure you have a backup system. (Remember, technology always fails at some point.) And check that the microphone is close enough to the story teller to capture everything being said. (I recommend monitoring your recording levels by using earphones.)

When recording stories for research, I suggest you stay away from using video unless there is a critical visual element in the story you need to capture. For example, someone might need to demonstrate how an item works—or walk you around a specific place. Remember, as the hero/designer of this story research, your goal is to discover hidden ideas and insights—not produce a viral marketing or promotional video. Video intimidates most people, so you'll get better stories without it.

Many folks simply take notes when collecting stories. This is fine—as long as you also record the stories some other way. I don't consider note-taking to be an appropriate, standalone recording method for this kind of qualitative research, as it doesn't capture the entire story for future review.

Right. Once you have your audio recorder fired up, how can you make sure you collect great stories with rich insights?

Shut up.

Seriously.

The key to good face-to-face story collection is listening. Ask your trigger question "Tell me about a time when you . . . ." Then stop talking. Clamp your lips together. Make eye contact with the story teller. Nod. Smile. Raise your eyebrows. And—

Keep. Your. Mouth. Shut.

Give the story teller time and space to think about what to say, to reflect, ponder, wander. Be. Patient. This is where the magic happens. This is where hidden intel and insights bubble up—in the space between sentences. And this is why story analysis generates much richer insight than any other form of qualitative research. If you're in a hurry—if you interrupt—if you jump on the end of a sentence—the story teller will sense that you're not really interested in what she's saying and will withdraw.

Try it. Ask a family member or coworker to tell you about a time she did x. Pick a positive experience. For example, the best trip she ever took. The first thing you'll notice is that, as soon as she starts talking, her story will trigger your own memories of similar experiences. You'll have a burning urge to interrupt her. To share your own story. To seek a connection and bond with her over shared experience. Shut it down. And shut up. I can't say this enough. Stay quiet. You can make time later to share your story. This activity is not about you. Has nothing to do with you. It is about her. About learning from—and honoring—her experience.

While you're listening, make mental notes about any gaps or incomplete story beats that intrigue you. Remember the 4D hero's design cycle of define, dream, dare, discover? Often when we're telling stories, we start to describe what we did during one cycle, then get interrupted and jump to another. If your story teller doesn't complete an important cycle, make a mental note to ask about it. If you don't trust your memory, write notes instead—though try not to distract her.

If you do a great job of shutting up, you'll likely only need to ask the first question to trigger a complete, compelling and interesting story. When the story teller pauses and you think she might be finished, keep your mouth shut. Count to ten. Let her think. Let the story breathe. Most of the time, she will start talking again, with additional details. Now you're past the obvious. Now things are going to get interesting.

Once you're certain that she has finished, you can break your silence. First, thank her for sharing that experience. Then, you can ask some follow-up questions to fill in the gaps. Assume that you have limited time with the story teller so ask your most important questions first. Another pro tip is to focus on what you need to learn to make sense of the problem—not what interests you most personally. It's easy to get distracted by our own emotions and passions here. Park them and focus on figuring out the design problem at hand.

If you're conducting a face-to-face group story collection, you probably won't be able to record all the stories in their entirety. For this work, I'd suggest giving everyone a structured form for note-taking that's based on the questions in the Story Canvas. Or give them mini versions of the Canvas to use as notepaper. Ask them to do their best to capture the key details of each story that's told. If there's time, they can review and revise their notes with the story tellers. At the end, collect these sheets for later analysis.

STORY RECORDING: VIA TECHNOLOGY

As new technologies continue to emerge daily, I can't possibly offer a comprehensive guide to tech-based story recording here. Instead, let's look at two of my favorite methods. You can adapt and evolve these for your own use.

Paper: The easiest thing to do is to print the Story Canvas and ask the story teller to fill in the blanks. With a bit of guidance, delivered in a workshop or on an instruction sheet, most people can do this easily. Even if the stories are short, filling in the quest is a great way to make experience and expertise explicit. We often don't know the details of what we do or why we do it. This forces us to walk through it intentionally. The process of having to fill in the boxes triggers reflection and analysis. What was I really trying to do in that story? Why? What was my purpose?

Though some people prefer to complete the Canvas on their own, I find that most do better working in pairs. That way, they can interview or prompt each other to tease out ideas that might not be obvious.

Another way to use the Canvas in groups is to record multiple stories on one canvas. Use sticky notes for each key story beat so that you can easily sort and cluster them. This sets you up nicely for a group analysis of all the stories shared.

If I'm helping a group with problem definition, I'll print a banner-size Canvas that we can put on the wall. We'll work through the questions as a group to capture the shared story of what has happened up to that point. Then we can analyze this to identify insights and ideas for next steps.

Online: I've also had great success creating online story "wizards" via web forms and survey software. Essentially, I take the questions in the Canvas and create a step-by-step form for people to complete that guides them through the process of telling their stories. The beautiful thing about this technology approach is that most survey tools automatically send the answers people submit directly to a spreadsheet.

So, the technology organizes your story data for analysis in real time. You can use this same approach to collect stories for a developmental evaluation research project. The spreadsheet creates a running storyline that captures your efforts to resolve the problem as they occur in real time. Over the course of a long project, the team reviews and analyzes the storyline regularly, to identify patterns, trends, insights and ideas.

Big and small organizations around the world use similar approaches to online story collection. Most focus on customers and users. Sadly, most are also poorly designed and executed—largely because the folks creating them don't understand the power of story data to generate intel and insights. They spend gobs of money to capture millions of generic user stories and republish a few of the most extraordinary. Then they abandon or trash the rest.

I see these story recording projects as the biggest missed opportunity of our time. The story databanks these organizations create are packed with untapped intel, insights and ideas. All someone needs to do is analyze and activate them for future innovations.

Story collection tips

It doesn't matter if I'm working face-to-face or over a satellite—I love collecting stories. Having someone trust and honor me enough to open up and share her personal experience is an incredibly precious gift. I'm also insatiably curious and never tire of hearing people's unique stories.

I've been fortunate to collect more than ten thousand stories over the past thirty-five years, working in a dozen languages, across five continents, in environments from igloos to spaceships. Here are the top eight things I learned:

1. **Listen.** Keep your mouth shut. Period. I can't say this enough. This is the oldest and most important rule of journalism that still holds today.

2. **Be patient.** Few of us can tell great stories off the top of our heads. We need time to reflect, remember, ruminate. Wait for it. The gold will come.

3. **Be appreciative.** Invite positive stories. Negative stories only reveal what is NOT working. They rarely offer insights into what's working well and how things could be even better—the kind of intel you need to innovate.

4. **Be specific.** Focus on actual experiences. Stories make abstract ideas real, tangible. Details matter.

5. **Ask why.** Do this enough and you'll uncover the real problem and purpose.

6. **Stay neutral.** Avoid embedding assumptions and bias in your questions.

7. **Stay open.** Never ask a yes-or-no question. When in doubt, ask why.

8. **Be curious.** This isn't about you. Curb your enthusiasm to share your own experience.

The only thing that's more rewarding than collecting stories is analyzing them. Unpacking them. Taking time to explore, rewind, repeat and relive someone's most extraordinary experience—and learning something new every single time I do it—generates the kind of paradigm-shifting insights you have to experience to believe.

3. ANALYZE STORIES.

At the end of your story collection process, you'll be left with a bunch of story recordings. Typically—and despite your best intentions to be organized—these will be a mess. Long, rambling audio files. Scribbles of notes across multiple notebooks. Heaps of incoherent stickies. Half-filled tables and forms. A stack of torn and stained Canvases.

It might not look like much, but this mess of stories is also a mess of raw, untapped data. Rich intel about problems, solutions, decisions and human behavior that can help you fuel your innovation project. Making sense of this intel and transforming it into useful insights and ideas is the heart of story analysis—the final step of your story research project.

What is analysis?

Story analysis is the process of deconstructing one or more stories in a methodical way. Breaking them down into bits and pieces to see how they operate in order to identify their problems, the activities of their heroes and the success or failure of their resolutions.

It's where you roll up your sleeves and dive into the details of the stories you've collected. It's sorting. Organizing. Comparing. Contrasting. To discover what worked and what didn't. Where stories are the same—and different. What mad risks paid off—and when things blew up.

Story analysis is sense-making. Your narrative intelligence at work. It's what you do to cut through all the complexity and crap of your situation—to figure out what's really happening. Why it's happening. And why it matters to the world.

Story analysis is also A-ha! land. Where inspiration bubbles, and ideas break through. Where genuinely new insights emerge and smack us in the forehead. Where jumbles of words, numbers and images suddenly take shape and form—and their meaning becomes clear.

It's where you analyze the data hidden in the stories you collected to generate useful intel, insights and ideas about real human behavior that are grounded in lived experience. That are directly relevant to your work. That you can use right now to move your innovation forward.

All from the comfort of your chair. Can you tell how much I love it?!

How to do an analysis

Story analysis can seem complex and overwhelming—especially if you've collected a lot of stories. It's easy to get distracted and lost in all the details. As always, the key is to stay focused on the question you're trying to answer. That is, uncovering insights and ideas that can help your story design or innovation project.

To do that, you really only need to accomplish one thing here: find patterns. How are the stories similar? And how are they different? These patterns (called "themes" by qualitative researchers) indicate trends in human behavior that can inform your design and decision-making.

You already have the narrative intelligence you need to be able to tease out these story patterns. You just need to organize all your story data in a way that makes it easy for you to see them. (Qualitative researchers call this "coding.")

The Story Canvas helps with this work. By giving you a place to organize your stories, you can sort and work with your data in a holistic way that enables you to spot patterns quickly and easily.

Though researchers all have personal preferences about how to work with their data, this is my general approach:

1. Organize your stories.
2. Review your story data to find common themes.
3. Review your stories again to find (unexpected) outliers.
4. Synthesize your findings into the most significant intel, insights and ideas.

When you break down these steps, the process goes something like the one below. Note that this approach describes how to do a methodical, sit-down story analysis, typically with one person. I'll describe how to do a live group analysis at the end of this section.

1. **Organize your stories.** This can be simple or complex, depending on how organized you were during story collection and what recording format you used. If you now have a bunch of audio or video recordings, I strongly suggest transcribing them—or, at the very least, listening to them and taking detailed notes. The good news is that you can now use artificial intelligence (AI) or automatic transcription software to do much of this work. (Pro tip: That's why you double checked the sound levels of all your audio recordings—to make sure they were good enough for your AI software to use.) If you have handwritten notes, you'll likely find that you'll need to get them typed up. Though this is often the easiest way to take notes in the field when collecting stories, it's the least useful for analysis. My recommendation? Get a little keyboard for your smartphone and get typing during your story collection.

Some people choose to put their transcripts into a text document; others like spreadsheets. Though I'm not particularly proficient with programming spreadsheets, I am slowly developing a preference for them, as they make it easier to sort and move chunks of text.

Once you transcribe your stories, you need to organize the content of each story into categories. This is where the Story Canvas comes into play. Each box on the Canvas works like a story category. So you can use the Canvas in a number of ways to organize your story data.

If you only have a few stories, I'd suggest transferring highlights of each story to the Canvas. You can use one Canvas per story. Or record multiple story highlights on one canvas. Use colored sticky notes (or markers) to represent different stories. This is my preferred method because you can then see data from multiple stories at a glance. You can also draw images and symbols as your own kind of shorthand to tell the stories. If you work on a banner-size Canvas, multiple people can work with the data at once, which can provide even more powerful insights.

If you don't want to work with paper versions of the Canvas, you can put a digital image of the canvas into any number of software programs, then use it as a background and add notes over top. I find this a little more awkward—though it does allow sharing of Canvases across distance.

You can also use the Canvas categories to create a table in a text document (Problem, Quest, etc.). Then you can organize your data according to the problem, purpose, quest and so on.

STORY CANVAS™ SPREADSHEET

TITLE:	HERO:		X-FACTOR:	
	Quest:			
Problem:	Define:	Define:	Define:	Define:
	Dream:	Dream:	Dream:	Dream:
Purpose:	Dare:	Dare:	Dare:	Dare:
	Discover:	Discover:	Discover:	Discover:
Resolution:	Intel:	Insights:		Ideas:

MY CURRENT FAVORITE APPROACH is to use the Canvas as a framework to create a spreadsheet-based story database. You can do this in any spreadsheet program, creating columns for different steps within the quest. The advantage to this is that you can break down and record multiple stories in one place. You can color-code different rows or columns. You can tag stories. And you can sort the rows according to different criteria.

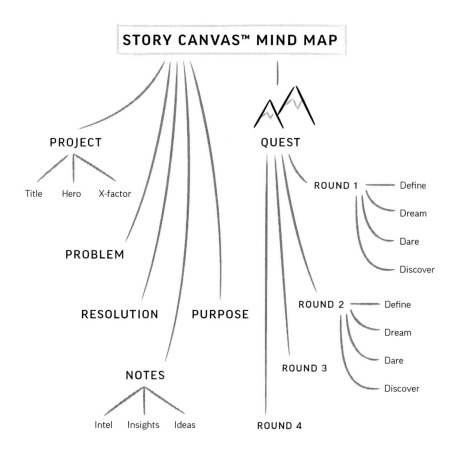

You can also use the Canvas categories and structure to create an online mind map or concept map of your story data like the one on page 117. This works best when you have brief notes as data (rather than detailed transcripts). A few benefits of this approach are that you can easily change and move the concept nodes or bubbles as you start your analysis. The nodes also collapse and expand, which helps you create useful snapshots of the data. You can use colors and shapes to organize data, which makes it easier to see patterns in a visual story map. And many online mind map apps allow you to share your work with others.

2. **Review all the stories and note common themes.** This is where the fun begins. Once you've organized your stories, it's time to start to unpack, study, analyze and reflect on them. You're going to spend time reviewing all your story data to see what you can learn.

During your first pass through the stories, you'll be looking for patterns: repeated sequences, arrangements or structures of events, activities or outcomes. So, you're really focused on repetition. And on action. What people do in the stories.

As a quick example, if you've collected stories about what people like to eat on Friday nights, when you review your stories, you might discover that most people go out or order in takeout food. This is a pattern. Flag it as you go over your data. You'll make sense of it—find out why—later.

When looking for patterns, I find it works best to use colors and tags to flag recurring items as I work through my story data. It doesn't really matter what system you use as long as you have a system and are consistent throughout your analysis. You might find that the three questions below work well as a way of identifying themes or patterns in your stories.[6]

a. **What happens? This is your intel.** Try to stick to just the facts here—don't read into what happened yet. What important observations can you make about the stories? What patterns stand out as similar across the stories? Are the problems all similar? Do the heroes do similar things? Do they make common mistakes? Run into the same obstacles all the time? What works well to help them succeed? Are the resolutions always the same?

b. So what? These are your insights. What do you think your observations mean? What are the implications of the patterns you see? If the hero faces the same problem in every story, can you learn from that? What does it mean if she fails at the same point in the quest every time? What inspiration can you find in the way she resolves the problems?

c. Now what? These are your ideas. This is where you let your insights spark your imagination. How might you build on this intel and these insights in your own work? What new ideas do these patterns trigger? Can you take something the hero does and transfer that story resolution to a different and related problem?

Once you're done this review, I recommend taking a break of at least a day. Let the intel and insights bubble in your mind. Be prepared to note ideas triggered by your reflections and analysis. Then, go back to the data for your next round of analysis.

3. **Review all the stories again and note outliers.** In your second review of the stories, you're looking for surprises. Which stories go against the trend? What did the hero do that you didn't expect? What things happened seemingly out of the blue? This is actually the most important part of the process for innovation because this is where you find fresh intel and inspiration—stuff you could never dream of. Use the three questions below to guide your review of the story data. And set up a system of color-coding and tagging that's different from the one you used in round one.

a. What happens? (Intel) What does the hero do differently to resolve problem? What unexpected things happen to her?

b. So what? (Insights) What are the implications of these differences? What insights do the outliers inspire? What can you learn from them?

c. Now what? (Ideas) What could these kinds of fringe or extreme actions mean for your work? What new ideas do they trigger?

4. **Synthesize your findings into the most significant intel, insights and ideas.** At this point, you want to start to move away from ground zero—the very specific detail of each individual story—and start to zoom up a few thousand feet in order to distill your findings into useful intel, insights and ideas. Can you cluster, group or generalize what you've seen in your patterns? Remember that you're doing this analysis for a reason—you want to use this work to guide next steps in your project. So, focus on what is useful, applicable, relevant. I suggest organizing your findings into the three categories of innovation information introduced above: intel, insight and ideas.

   When you do this, be sure to show how they are related. You'll need to help others understand the source of your ideas, to show that they are grounded in evidence contained in your story data. Your intel should reveal a specific pattern—to inform an insight about the way people behave—which sparks an idea about how to change that behavior. This analytical trail is helpful for sharing your ideas and can inform logic models for funders and stakeholders.

   At the end of this process, you'll have distilled hours of story data into a few key actionable insights about what worked well to resolve the story problems. You'll also have generated ideas about how those resolutions can inform your own innovation quest.

INDIVIDUAL OR GROUP ANALYSIS?

As we've seen, anyone can do a story analysis. All you need is time—and stories! Deciding which approach to take depends on your project budget, timeline, story tellers and, ultimately, your research question—what you need to learn through the analysis.

Individuals. If you will be the primary user of the intel generated, you should do the analysis yourself. This is the most informative and most resource-intensive approach. If you don't have time—or you'd like a more objective analysis—you can hire a professional to do the analysis for you. In general, I'd recommend that both story collection and analysis be done by the same person. Even if you recorded everything that was said or done during a story analysis, we all remember other details, like facial expression and body language, that can add to our analysis. If your analyst wasn't there during the recording, she won't be able to include these kinds of observations in her work.

Groups. Typically, one or more "trained professionals" will analyze all the stories. Most traditional academic inquiry and market research methods tend to focus on classic interview approaches: one interviewer with one or more subjects. However, methods in which groups share and analyze their own stories can generate extremely rich data.

Why? Because this method benefits from access to each group member's unique narrative intelligence "lens," which she applies to analyze each story.

Remember, we all have narrative intelligence. And we all have a lifetime of experience analyzing stories.

If your research method uses only one person—one researcher—to analyze a collection of stories about a specific topic, then you will yield only one interpretation of those stories' meaning; one person is analyzing the story data through a single, personal lens of experience—her own unique lifetime story database. Her narrative intelligence analysis "lens" is limited to what she knows.

Now, if you invite ten people to share stories methodically and you get all ten of them to analyze all ten stories methodically, then you'll tap into ten different lifetime story databases and produce one hundred different analyses. That means that you'll increase the odds of discovering new ideas and intel ten times.

THIS KIND OF participatory research method also generates several other key benefits. Most importantly, since no one person has the solution to a complex, wicked problem, this approach enables systemic change by mobilizing expertise across communities of interest. It also empowers stakeholders by explicitly placing value on their expertise and experience. Finally, listening to and analyzing stories builds individual critical-thinking expertise—an essential skill in growing capacity for resilience and innovation.

Group Analysis. You can scale your group analysis in many ways, depending on the size of your project and number of participants. I tend to use one of two approaches: a small group or a large group of pairs.

Small group. In a small group, invite participants to share stories and give each person one Story Canvas to capture the highlights of the stories they hear. This works best if you have time to provide some coaching and tips before they start. You might want to spend a few minutes introducing them to basic story structure, using the Story Specs. Then, walk them through the Story Canvas briefly so they can see how it works. Give them hints on what to listen for, such as similarities and differences between stories, surprises and outliers and things that worked well to resolve the story problems. Using the boxes of the Canvas to gather problems, resolutions and quest actions for multiple stories will naturally help them start to see patterns.

Once everyone has shared a story, facilitate a live story analysis. Use the questions from the analysis process above to guide the group. First, look for patterns and similarities, then outliers.

Record their answers on a banner-size Story Canvas on the wall, using color-coded sticky notes. What trends did they see in the problems, quests, resolutions? What outliers did they notice? Once you've captured all their responses, ask them to help you sort, cluster, distill and synthesize the intel, insights and ideas on the sticky notes. Aim for six to eight key ideas as your final outcome.

Large group. If you're working with a larger group, it's not practical to share all the stories with the entire group. Instead, give everyone a crash course in story collection and analysis as described above. Then, invite them to work in pairs. Each person shares a story and the other captures it on the Story Canvas. At that point, you can have them share their intel, insights and ideas with the larger group. Or, if it's a really big crowd, add an intermediate step. Bring the pairs together into small groups to distill their findings, then bring the small groups into the big group.

The downside of this approach is that only one person gets to hear and analyze each story. So you don't benefit from multiple lenses during the analysis. However, this is a tremendously powerful way of

PARTICIPATORY STORY ANALYSIS
INTEL GENERATED BY TEN ANALYSTS VS. ONE

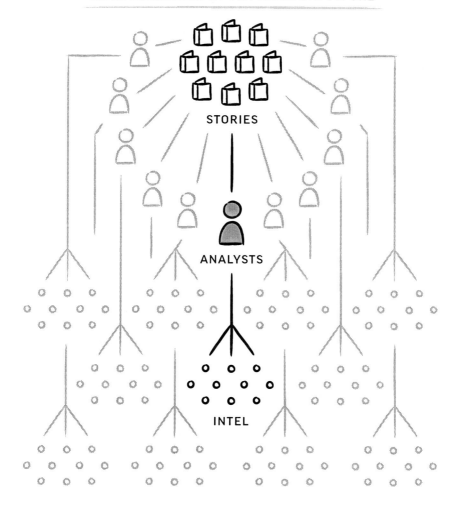

STORIES

ANALYSTS

INTEL

both mobilizing masses of experience and engaging people in generating ideas toward a shared problem.

Benefits

Once you start to use story research in your work, you'll understand why I say it's the most powerful innovation tool in the world. No other method can deliver benefits like these.

1. INSTANT AND USEFUL RESULTS.

The moment you start working with stories, your narrative intelligence starts to produce new knowledge and information that you can use across your innovation project.

- You develop intel that's grounded in lived experience to inform design and decision-making.

- You develop unexpected insights about the diverse, real-world problems of others.

- You develop unique ideas, informed by story-based intel and insights.

- You make abstract concepts from big data specific and real.

- You discover hidden knowledge and skills relevant to your work.

- You find proven resolutions to existing problems.

- You generate evidence of program and strategic impact.

- You enrich your own story bank with experiences that are easy to remember and share.

2. FAST AND EASY APPROACH.

You can do story research anywhere, anytime, about any topic, with anyone. I've done projects where we generated comprehensive design criteria for a new business in less than fifteen minutes through a group story analysis.

3. STRATEGIC ENGAGEMENT.

Story research is a participatory activity that brings the added benefits of engagement to your project. By inviting people to share—and sometimes help you analyze—stories, you're implicitly creating additional value for your work.

- You acknowledge people's experience and expertise.
- You nurture new and existing relationships.
- You create a way for people to join you on your quest to resolve a problem.
- You empower people to take ownership of the problem and future resolutions.

That's it. Now that you've deconstructed a bunch of stories to find your big idea, all you need to do to complete your innovation project is bring it to life. Time to flip from story research to story design.

Story Design
An Innovation Driver

W E'VE ALREADY SPENT some time on design theory and process. So this part should be pretty straightforward, right? Nail down your problem, sketch out your quest and off you go. Piece of cake.

Except that any designer who's been around the block can tell you that design processes never, ever go as planned. That's why you need a design tool that guides you through the fun and often frustrating work of making your idea tangible, trying it out in the real world, watching what happens and revising it until it works.

In the last chapter, you learned to use the Story Canvas to take stories—or designs—apart. How to *deconstruct* and analyze them. This chapter flips that process and shows you how to use your narrative intelligence and the Canvas to *construct* or create stories, experiences and strategies. How to translate what's in your head into a tangible solution to your problem. How to give shape to, test and refine big ideas into innovations that help you realize your purpose.

Just a side note: Although I'm treating research and design as two separate activities here, they're often not. As mentioned, it might seem logical in theory to do your research first, which would generate fresh intel, insights and ideas about what might work to resolve your problem. Then, you'd stop researching and use your findings to guide your design quest to create a resolution.

In practice, the process is rarely as neat or linear as that. Once you get into the work of design, you may discover that you need ongoing research to produce new intel to answer new questions you encounter along the way. And you'll need to design new research activities to explore and evaluate your work. So don't be surprised if you find yourself alternating between story research (collecting and deconstructing stories) and story design (constructing and refining resolutions).

4D story design cycle

As we learned in Part One, design is essentially a problem-solving process. An iterative cycle of creative and analytical activities that generates a proven resolution to a new kind of problem. Though creatives like writers, painters, musicians and innovators each have unique processes for design, we all go through these same basic steps, no matter the kind of problem we face.

In this book, we're using the 4D story design cycle. That's the same process you explored earlier, where each QUEST box in the Story Canvas represents one story beat or mini-design cycle within the overall project quest. Remember what each D in the 4D story design cycle refers to:

DEFINE (Now what?)
Hero uses insights to (re)define the *problem*.

DREAM (What if?)
Hero imagines resolutions and generates an *idea*.

DARE (What happens?)
Hero tries idea and observes what happens to produce *intel*.

DISCOVER (So what?)
Hero analyzes intel to develop *insights*.

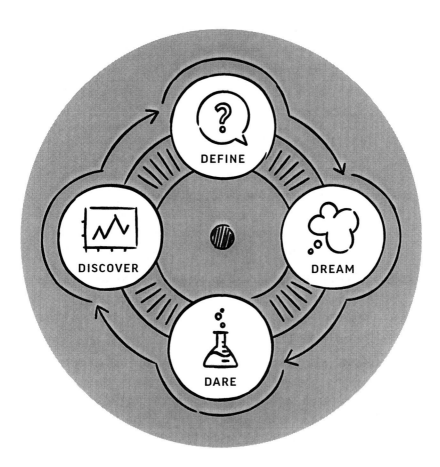

On paper, every different design process—including this one—looks nice, neat and logical. Easy-to-follow steps, like footprints on the floor of a dance studio. In real life, though, when you're in the middle of a crisis, you often rip through the different parts of a design process subconsciously, automatically, in nanoseconds.

As a result, you can make terrible choices about how to resolve the problem. Using the Canvas as a guide to story design helps you slow the process down and makes each step deliberate so you can make sure each step is also awesome. This, in turn, makes sure your design resolution or innovation is equally awesome. This commitment to being intentional is a key attribute and benefit of working through a set design process.

BENEFITS

Why use story as your design framework instead of some other business or creative approach? We've already revealed the power of narrative intelligence, as our innate ability to make sense of and design resolutions to problems through the lens of story.

Now, as we get into the specifics of design, we discover a few additional benefits of using story as your main method for problem-solving and innovation.

- **Story design is disruptive.** People need triggers to innovate. They need to be disrupted. Every story design cycle embeds triggers that force design heroes to challenge the status quo and try something new. This is a requirement for innovation.

- **Story design engages stakeholders.** Unlike traditional consultations, meetings, presentations and endless email chains, the process of designing through story gives people something concrete to do. They become heroes in the quest. Story design gets people involved in framing problems, creating resolutions and sharing their success. We engage in story design to resolve problems related to strategy and service in (almost) the exact same way we engage with a movie hero as she resolves her problem.

- **Story design is cyclical, iterative.** Remember, every quest the hero takes is actually a series of cycles or story beats made up of the 4Ds. In each cycle, the hero tests an idea to see if it will resolve her problem. As she progresses in her quest, she goes through multiple cycles, testing a new idea every time, until at last one of them works and she reaches a resolution. (Or she dies trying!) Iterating through the process is key to making sure she designs the right resolution for the right problem.

- **Story design is reflective.** Every story beat cycle includes a step in which the hero reflects on what she has done so far to resolve her problem and how well her ideas have worked so she can figure out what to do next. (What if? What happens? So what? Now what?) Though reflection is something we rarely do intentionally in real life, it's an essential part of effective design. That's why expert designers build reflection activities into their processes.

- **Story design is deliberate.** Intentionality is a defining characteristic of design. When we start to design something, we seek to resolve a specific problem. So, every single thing we do as part of that process should contribute to creating the best resolution possible. Nothing happens by accident in design. Every decision is made for a reason. We define problems, dream up ideas, dare to try them out and discover insights deliberately, with a view to resolving the problem. As a result, we don't waste resources. And we get resolutions that are crafted explicitly to address specific problems.

- **Story design is comprehensive.** It guides you through the entire innovation process.

- **Story design is fun.** It's a social activity that strengthens relationships and enables you to benefit from the diverse perspectives of multiple participants.

- **Story design is agile, affordable and accessible.** Anyone can use the process described in this book anywhere, anytime, to resolve (almost) any kind of problem.

Uses

In fact, I think of story design as the ultimate multitool for innovation. Any time you need to resolve a problem, story design can work.

I know. It can be tough at first to think of things like strategies, experiences and service as stories. That's because our rational, logical scientific biases have all but obliterated our ability to use other forms of intelligence (e.g., narrative, emotional, creative and interpersonal) to make decisions and lead change. Maybe these explanations will help.

A *strategy* is essentially a plan. It describes how you (and your people) will achieve one or more shared goals. To design your plan, you'll need to define your purpose (*why* your strategy matters), problem (*what* obstacles you need to overcome to succeed) and quest (*how* you plan to do it). Note that a campaign is pretty much the same thing; it's a plan to get people to do something.

An *experience* is the unfolding of a story. Remember from Part One that a story describes a hero's experience solving a problem. When you design an experience, you're designing activities through which people will solve a problem. The experience could be anything. A trade show, where your boss needs to test a new product. A shopping trip, where the customer needs to buy something. A hospital visit, where the patient needs medical care. A smartphone interaction, where the user needs to send a message. A meal out, where patrons need a quiet place to eat and talk.

Note that *service* and *experience* design are closely linked. As a service provider, you design a service that creates an experience for your customer. What you call this design depends on where you focus—on what the provider does or what the customer experiences. The practice of experience design is relatively new to the mainstream and worth exploring further as a powerful way to create change and achieve impact. Check out some of the work published by and about Disney to learn more.[1]

If you use story design as your framework for experience design, you not only create a great experience but you also make it easy for people to remember and share their experience. That's because you develop the experience as a customer story: "Best meal ever"; "Incredible start to my new job"; "Quick thinking saved my life."

Unfortunately, we rarely take the time to design everyday experiences deliberately, to achieve a specific purpose or resolve a problem.

Instead, we leave the design of most experiences—like sales meetings and elevator rides—to chance. Remember, people have to have an experience to change. If your design problem is to change the way people think or act (and it probably is, to some degree), you might want to consider putting more effort into designing the experiences you use to trigger that change. That means deliberately designing everything from large events to one-on-one conversations, from individual workspaces to community transit services.

Finally, it's worth remembering that a *story* itself is a communication tool that also needs to be designed to resolve a specific problem. All messages, all media need to have a goal, a purpose. And you need to design your stories explicitly to meet those goals.

Over the past few years, I've used story design to create strategies, experiences, services and more to help clients who needed to solve problems like these:

- Change national policy for the treatment of posttraumatic stress disorder.

- Engage a global aerospace team in pursuit of a new mission.

- Create a campaign to win a patent required to launch a new sports drink.

- Define purpose for a growing leadership consultancy.

- Reduce chronic disease among South Asian immigrants.

- Evaluate ongoing development of a low-barrier employment service.

- Redesign the business model of an academic publisher.

It doesn't really matter what specific problem you're facing. Story design works as an agile design framework to help you create resolutions to all kinds of challenges—from communication and strategy to research and evaluation. Got it?

Perfect. Let's get you working like a designer.

Example

You'll find it easier to work through story design with the Story Canvas if you have a project or venture to use for practice. In this section, I'm going to use the sxd (Student Experience Design) online learning project I referenced earlier as an example. You can see a working version of the sxd Canvas on page 138.

For context, here's a project snapshot:

sxd started out as a one-day design studio for twenty-five online postsecondary students in Ontario, sponsored by a not-for-profit agency called eCampusOntario (eco), the postsecondary online learning portal for the province of Ontario (Canada). During the studio, I led the students through a condensed version of my story design process, using a banner-size version of the Story Canvas to explore ways that students could make online learning in Ontario even better. After just seven hours, the students had produced a series of solution prototypes, which they shared at a faculty showcase event the following day. This initial work served as the foundation for what is now the sxd Lab, a province-wide student experience design innovation lab led by and for students. Funded by eco, the sxd Lab is the first of its kind in Canada—possibly the world.

Though in hindsight the project story sounds nice, neat and straightforward, it didn't start this way—which is why I want to use it as an example of how story design can guide and shape your innovation journey. In fact, sxd began with a direct message on Twitter from a colleague who had just stepped into a new role as the CEO of eCampusOntario. Our original tweet chat went like this:

CEO: What are you up to these days? Curious about your trajectory.

DW: Self-employed innovation consultant—using story as an R&D framework to lead change in public & social sectors. Plus writing a how-to playbook. Largely driven by my SFU engagement and narrative research. How's Toronto?

CEO: Crowded but lively. Lots of headroom for doing interesting stuff.

DW: Online innovation ed. is booming (with IDEO leading this space). Happy to chat if you ever want to bounce ideas around.

CEO: I've already signaled Ministry and others that we want to do an IDEO-style design workshop with students in January 2017 to push the need for better styles of online courses that engage student learning, thinking, co-creation, etc. Think about it . . .

DW: Face-to-face or online for the Jan. workshop? Lots of ideas we could discuss. (I've taught this a few times—also co-created the original curriculum and studio space for Sauder d.studio.) Will put my thinking hat on . . .

CEO: FTF. In Toronto at the new Toronto Public Library space at Bloor/Yonge. Lovely space.

DW: Cool. I used to hang out at the old library there—haven't seen the new one. I'll think about it and follow up next week.

CEO: Alright then. Think it over and we can chat next week.

Can you spot the problem? The purpose? No? Don't worry—neither could I. That's why this is a great example for our story design practice. It's messy and complex, so it's representative of the kind of real-world work you might be doing. And—at the time I'm writing this—it's very much still in progress. So, you can get a sense of how innovation evolves and emerges throughout the design process.

As we work through this section, I'll also use jet packs as a design process example to demonstrate some of the trickier concepts—just because they're fun—and a bit more concrete than the SXD Lab.

METHOD

Ready?

First, grab a fresh blank Canvas. Looks great, doesn't it?

Actually, I always find that it looks a little terrifying. Some might say downright intimidating. Because it doesn't matter if you're a painter or innovator, a blank canvas can paralyze the most experienced designer. It just sits there, screaming "White space!" in your face, daring you to be brilliant. Where should you start? How should you start?

Here's one of the first rules of design. When you're stuck, just do something. Anything. It doesn't matter what you do—taking action deliberately will get you unstuck. Kind of like getting the first scratch on a new car. Once it's no longer perfect, you can relax and enjoy it.

If you're feeling bold, go for it. Write or draw on the Canvas. Anything, anywhere. If you want to play it a little safe, start by filling in your name.

Done? There. You ARE brilliant. Now, keep going with the easy stuff—just like tackling a tough exam. Do what you know first and build some momentum from there. What's your project title? Easy.

HERO

Great. Now, name your hero.

Hmm. As we saw in the tour of the Story Canvas earlier, this is another part that can be obvious or tricky, depending on your project. If you're using story design to resolve a real-world problem—to innovate or create something new—you (and your team) are likely playing the role of hero/designer. You'll be the one using your sword-fighting skills to slay dragons, climb mountains and find treasure in pursuit of your purpose.

On the other hand, if you're designing a story to share, which describes someone else's experience, then you should make that person the hero. This works particularly well when working with customer or user stories. Everything you design is created for the sole purpose of resolving a problem, right? If your design (product, service, experience, strategy) helps someone else resolve a problem, then that person is the hero. You and your resolution are simply sidekicks that help out in a specific manner.

Another way to think about this is to realize that your resolution only exists because of that customer or hero. If she didn't have an unmet need or problem to resolve, you'd have no reason to design. Your user's need is your innovation's raison d'être. For example, if my Story Canvas helps you innovate, then you are the hero of that innovation, not me. I'm the sidekick. I'm going to tell the story of how you innovated—with my support.

Bottom line: If you're resolving your own problem, you are the hero. If you're helping someone else resolve her problem, she is the hero.

SXD Example

For the SXD project, my clients started out as the hero and I helped them lead the experience design quest for the initial one-day design studio. As the project evolved and the quest grew, we gradually engaged hundreds of students, staff, faculty and leaders from across Ontario. Today, the SXD Lab has teams of hero/designers across the province, all working to solve multiple and diverse problems—yet all focused on achieving the same purpose.

X-FACTOR

Next, what's the X-factor? What makes this story or innovation extraordinary? Your X-factor might be obvious—something like access to an alien technology. Or you might not know yet. And that's okay. The next design rule is that there are no right answers. So just go with your gut for now. Guess—or put down something wild and crazy that you'd love to have as your X-factor. Because I don't know exactly how the power of intention works, but there is something wondrous about stating your desires out loud. Making your goals real and putting them out there. Often, the universe finds a way to make them happen.

If that feels too "magical" for you, add your desired X-factor for this reason instead—you have nothing to lose by writing down a hunch, a desire, a stretch goal. Remember, the Canvas is nothing more than a worksheet. You can change and discard it at any time. Don't be afraid to add and remove content as often as you like.

SXD Example

For the SXD Lab, the X-factor was and still is a commitment to student-led innovation. As noted earlier, historically, everything to do with

TITLE	HERO
SXD (Student Experience Design) Lab	eCampusOntario

PROBLEM
If we can enable student-led innovation—

PURPOSE
—then we can make online learning even better.

DEFINE
NOW WHAT?

How might we figure out a way to tackle this giant problem?

How might we resolve each of the mini-problems?

DREAM
WHAT IF?

What if— eCampusOntario hosts a one-day design jam for students to see how student-led innovation could work?

What if—students use future stories to envision, develop and test resolutions?

DARE
WHAT HAPPENS?

25 students travel to Toronto from across Ontario for the studio. First activity is to share stories of excellent online learning experiences.

In teams, students sketch ideas, then make and test prototypes of those ideas. E.g., include real-time simulation coaching during learning.

DISCOVER
SO WHAT?

Students analyze stories and identify mini-problems to work on.

Students generate 7 prototypes with real innovation potential in just one day.

INTEL

- Students often expect others to fix the problems they identify instead of taking the lead to do it themselves.
- Working asynchronously across distance was challenging.
- First 2 SXD events were sold out.

INSIGHTS

STORY CANVAS™

How might we share these ideas with others to engage them in our quest?	How might eco provide real-world support to the student teams to develop their prototypes?	How might we create a "container" to develop a model for sustainable student-led innovation?	**RESOLUTION** Still unknown.
What if we present the prototypes at an elearning showcase?	What if we invite elearning technology vendors to work with the students to develop the prototypes further?	What if we launch a virtual SXD (Student Experience Design) Lab for student-led innovation?	
All teams share their stories and prototypes with over 300 faculty and education leaders. Faculty keen to listen and ask lots of questions.	Recruit 4 global vendors and pair them with 4 student teams to develop prototypes and pitch them to 100+ students at an SXD Kickstart event.		
Audience seems interested—but not many "sign up" for future engagement. However, eCO sees potential and wants to explore more.	3/4 ideas have potential to go further. Not all vendors committed. eco keen to continue exploring student-led innovation.		

- Most students lack experience bringing ideas to life.
- Many students struggle to think big, differently, in the future.
- Faculty very excited to hear from "real" students. Don't they work with real students every day?

IDEAS

- Use the lab as a way to prototype a new kind of experiential learning opportunity.
- Extend SXD Lab nationally.
- Low-hanging fruit: faculty could simply engage their own students in co-creating courses and content.

postsecondary education has been developed, managed and "owned" by institutions, faculty, experts, the government. The sxd Lab empowers students, for the first time ever, to drive innovation to create the learning experiences they want and need.

PROBLEM

Defining your design problem clearly is the hardest and most important part of design. Period. Again, if you take nothing else from this book, remember that. You must know what problem you need to resolve before you can design a resolution that works. Remember the soup factory example? If you tell an architect to "build something over there," the first thing she'll do is to ask you what you want to use the building for.

When folks start an innovation project, they often start with an idea for a solution. Something they want to make because they think it'd be super cool. And it might be. The thing is, you run into trouble if you need people to choose to use it. Or—even more crazy—pay for it. Then, it's not enough for your innovation to be cool. It also has to create real, significant value for them if you want them to invest their precious time or money in it. Remember, every innovation has to have a value proposition. The way innovations create value for us is that they solve our problems. The good news is that a problem can be anything from feeling sad to having a heart attack to losing your car keys to slowing climate change.

We also now know from our earlier work that problem definition can be so tricky that it's unlikely you'll get it right on your first attempt. It's more likely that you'll have to revise and redefine it repeatedly throughout the design process. That's perfect—that's exactly what should happen. Better definitions lead to better resolutions.

Start by writing down the problem as you know it now—and go from there. You can revise it during the project. If you're really stuck and absolutely can't figure out a problem to start with, then you can try the following quick activity to see if it helps.

Five Whys

This is a pretty popular technique among the innovation crowd these days. Though you can use it a couple of different ways, I find it works best like this.

State your problem as best you can. Then have someone ask you why five times. For example:

Problem: The world needs emission-free jet packs.

1. Why does the world need emission-free jet packs?
   Because they'd be better than cars for personal transportation.

2. Why would they be better than cars for personal transportation?
   Because they'd be better for the environment.

3. Why would they be better for the environment?
   Because they'd run on renewable energy.

4. Why would renewable energy be better?
   Because it would slow climate change.

5. Why do we need to slow climate change?
   Because it's going to kill off the human race.

You can start to see a few giant issues emerging here. This problem statement is jammed with assumptions (instead of intel and insights). And it actually describes a resolution—not a problem. "Emission-free jet packs" are one resolution to the (giant) problem "How can we save the human race?"

This kind of problem-framing is super common in design and innovation. Almost every client I work with comes to me with a resolution, thinking it's a problem. "How can I design an emission-free jet pack for mass production?" Don't get me wrong—I love jet packs. But in this instance, I don't see that the client has done the work to figure out what problem she really needs to resolve. If she wants to save humans from extinction, there are many ways to do that. Jet packs might be one. And there might be a better resolution—which she would discover through a deliberate design process.

PROBLEM
If we can enable
student-led innovation–

SXD Example

Going back to the initial Twitter chat that launched SXD, it's obvious that we didn't have a clear problem to start with. We knew that students historically had not been part of learning design, programming or policy decisions in any meaningful way. And we knew that we wanted to change that. So, part of what we wanted to do during the one-day studio was start to define the problem. To do that, we needed to identify some initial opportunities to *empower students to lead innovation in online learning*—to do things differently. That's what I wrote in the PROBLEM box at the beginning.

PURPOSE

You're likely starting to see that your problem definition can be quite short and simple or messy and complex. The thing to remember is that your problem statement is just the beginning—just the first half of framing your project. That's because your problem has to connect to a purpose. What is the point of your design work? What do you need to change? Why are you doing this work?

Your purpose gives meaning to your project. It describes the ultimate outcome or impact. It tells us how the world will be different because of your innovation.

The good news is that figuring out your purpose is starting to get a bit easier, as more and more organizations work to articulate their purpose and align activities to achieve it.

On the flip side, lots of innovators struggle to state their purpose clearly, often skipping this part of the process altogether. In my experience, these tend to be the folks who are chasing predetermined resolutions. They confuse purpose and resolution. Designing the jet pack is their purpose.

While it might be okay to be fuzzy on your purpose at the beginning of your project, you are going to have to tackle this at some point. Because you're going to need to know why you're designing a jet pack if you ever want to sell it. So, just as you did with the problem, take your best shot at defining your purpose and write it in the box. You can and should update it as your project unfolds.

If–Then

Once you have your problem and your purpose, you can test them out to see if they make sense by putting them into an *If–then* statement that describes your future innovation or story in a short sentence.

If–then statements have been around forever and are common in research and science. Essentially, they state what you want to do and why it matters. You can think of an *If–then* statement as a hypothesis you want to test or a hunch you want to explore. I use the *If–then* approach a lot when I'm doing social innovation work as a way to generate simple *theory of change* statements. Forcing myself to frame my project this way ensures that I've done the work to figure out my problem and purpose *before* starting my quest.

If–then statements are also a great tool for revealing assumptions and weaknesses in your logic that can sabotage your project. This makes them extremely useful for projects that require logic models, as they provide an overall framework to describe what you're planning to do and why it matters.

Here's how an *If–then* statement works.

If *describes your problem (what you're trying to do).*

Then *describes your purpose (why this work matters and what will change if you succeed).*

Let's go back to the jet-pack example from the Five Whys exercise to see an example. Based on what we learned by unpacking that problem statement, we can now write this *If–then* statement as a theory of change.

If I *can design an emission-free jet pack for mass production,* then I *can save the human race from extinction via climate change.*

Logically, that statement works. Awesome. It's a great description to help people understand what you're trying to do and why it matters.

However, keep in mind that we also discovered that designing a jet pack is only one of many possible ways to achieve the purpose of saving the human race.

If I design solar roadways, then I can save the human race from extinction via climate change.

If I can harness tidal energy, then I can save the human race from extinction via climate change.

Need a few more examples?

If I can destroy the ring of power, then I can save the world from being overrun by the evil Sauron. (The Lord of the Rings)

If I can get back to Kansas, then I will always feel loved. (The Wizard of Oz)

If we can develop a malaria vaccine, then we can save lives.

Remember, as you work through your quest, your problem will likely shift and evolve. So don't get too attached to it. Innovation is all about purpose. Stay focused on why you're doing this work, as a way to guide decision-making during the quest.

PURPOSE
–then we can make online learning even better.

SXD Example

If we look at my SXD example, our project didn't have a stated purpose in the beginning, though we did have some hunches and big ideas about how we wanted to change the world. One of the first things I did was work with the ECO team to unpack these ideas and distill an initial purpose we could start with. I knew we would need something clear that we could all understand and support—otherwise, we'd never get the project off the ground.

After a few conversations, we chose this as our purpose: *Make online learning in Ontario even better.* Though this seems simple and obvious as a statement of purpose, it has stood the test of time and continues to function as a terrific target or beacon for us—a great way to check in to make sure we are still on track. It makes clear the user being served (students), and it makes clear what we want to change (online learning experiences). It also signals that we are already doing a lot of things well in this space.

Bringing our problem and purpose together, this is the theory of change that we started with:

> If we can empower students to lead innovation in online learning, then we can make online education in Ontario even better.

It's not fancy—and it does the trick.

Note that this statement deliberately focuses on the *what* and *why* of the project/venture—not the *how*. How is the work of the quest, which comes next.

This is where things get tricky. *Empowering students to lead innovation in online learning* is a giant, hairy system-change kind of problem. Much more complex than something like figuring out how to get my dog to stop chewing my slippers. (Though also a hairy problem!) And probably a lot like the kinds of problems you face. A problem so big that it's almost impossible to know where or how to start.

This is where most of my clients stall out. They sit and stare at the problem, overwhelmed by its complexity, uncertain what to do next. This is where you really start to think and work like a designer. This is where your quest begins.

QUEST

The good news is that you now have a sense of what problem you need to resolve, and why it matters. The bad news is that your problem is likely too big for you to resolve all in one go. How can we empower students to lead innovation in online learning? How can we save the human race from extinction due to climate change? These are wicked and complex problems. How do you get started?

You need to break down the problem and find one manageable chunk to start with. Then, you can use the structure of the quest on the Story Canvas to guide you through a deliberate, iterative, scalable process. Working methodically, step by step, you'll define small, workable problems, dream of ideas, dare to test those to produce intel and discover insights that ultimately lead you to a resolution.

Hmm. That doesn't sound like much of a crazy, chaotic or fun innovation adventure. It actually sounds kind of dull and pedantic, right? That's exactly right.

Launching an innovation quest can feel like stepping into an action-adventure movie. The exhilaration, creative rush and generative momentum can sweep you off your feet, tantalizing you with glimmers of your ultimate resolution—your happily ever after. It can be easy to get caught up in chasing dreams and hard to stay on track.

Having the discipline to slow down and work one step at a time is a key design skill—one that takes dedication and practice. You will be tempted to jump from idea to idea—to skip the hard work of testing, analyzing and reflecting on what is working (or not) and why. Don't.

If you do, you risk missing out on the deep learning that happens during the process. Rushing past the hidden intel, insights and ideas that can make or break your innovation.

This is why I designed the Story Canvas. I know that innovation is never neat, linear or straightforward. I also know that every project needs some structure—a path to follow, a recipe for success. The QUEST section of the Canvas gives you that deliberate, step-by-step design roadmap. Working through the iterative framework of the quest will help you stay on track, monitor progress and avoid getting overwhelmed by complexity and options. How? By activating your narrative intelligence.

As you work through the real-life experience—the story—of your unfolding design process, your narrative intelligence automatically kicks in. It starts to work in sync with the story design cycle naturally, easily. You'll start to think and problem-solve through the lens of story. You'll be able to analyze and makes sense of what is happening in real time. Find patterns and outliers. Identify intel, insights and ideas that trigger inspiration. Define, dream, dare and discover new opportunities that ultimately lead to breakthrough innovation.

But if you don't follow the process and do the work, if you skip steps and take shortcuts, you'll cheat yourself and your project. You'll miss out on the creative and critical-thinking benefits that only your narrative intelligence can bring.

Whew! That's it for my "stick to the process" lecture! On to the quest.

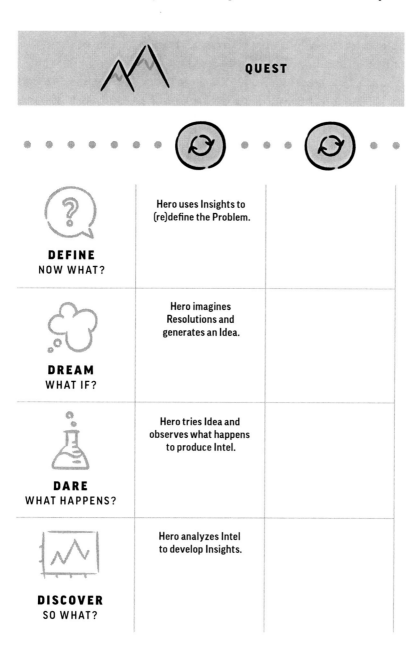

QUEST

DEFINE
NOW WHAT?

Hero uses Insights to (re)define the Problem.

DREAM
WHAT IF?

Hero imagines Resolutions and generates an Idea.

DARE
WHAT HAPPENS?

Hero tries Idea and observes what happens to produce Intel.

DISCOVER
SO WHAT?

Hero analyzes Intel to develop Insights.

When you look at the Story Canvas, you can see that I've divided the QUEST section into boxes. You can subdivide, add or group the boxes however you like. If you find the Canvas isn't big enough for your project, use multiple Canvases, create a banner or sketch an online version in a diagramming program.

Each box represents one complete story beat or mini-design cycle—a dot in the Story Specs™ arc from Part One. Each of these design cycles represents an effort by the hero to resolve the main story problem. In a way, each cycle functions a bit like a mini-story, complete with a mini-problem, mini-quest and mini-resolution. As we saw earlier, you can unpack each cycle even further to reveal the 4DS of story design. These 4DS form the backbone of the entire process. Once you learn how they work, you can control them from your captain's chair in the story design cockpit to manipulate the direction, pace, scope and impact of your innovation project.

DEFINE (NOW WHAT?)

One of the secrets to successful story design is finding ways to turn gnarly, gargantuan problems into small-scale, manageable questions. To identify one tiny part of your giant problem that you think you can tackle and begin there. It's a bit like doing a puzzle—you have to pick one specific piece to start with.

How do you know which piece is the right one? You don't. And you won't. Get over it. Remember what I said in Part One? Learning to live with ambiguity and uncertainty are essential design skills.

Once you let go of the need to find the one right answer, to pick the exact right problem to start with, you can relax and start to trust the process. Have faith in the work you've already done, in the work you're about to do. Think of this as a chance to ask yourself, "Now what? What should I do next?"

If you're stuck at the beginning, the easiest way to start is to go back to study the intel, insights and ideas you produced during your project story research. Identify any ideas that stand out as being rich in potential or barriers that you must address before doing anything

VARIABLE 1

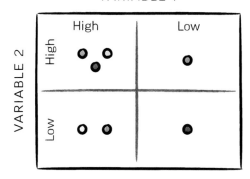

2×2 PRIORITY GRID

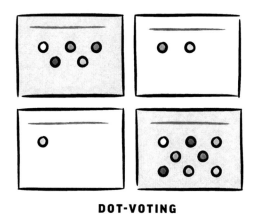

DOT-VOTING

CRITERIA

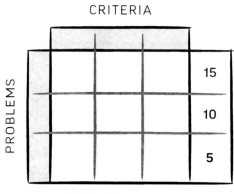

DECISION MATRIX

else. Then, sort these potential starting points, using a tool like a 2×2 priority grid,[2] dot-voting[3] or a decision matrix,[4] as illustrated on the previous page.

These kinds of sorting tools can help you narrow things down quickly and easily by using ranking criteria like "most likely to succeed," "easiest," "cheapest," "fastest," "highest impact," "most relevant." Work through one or more of these sorting activities to pick one idea that seems most likely to move your project forward, then define it as a new mini-problem to resolve. It's often easiest to frame it like this: "*How might we—?*"

Once you have your mini-problem or challenge, add it to the first Define box of the QUEST. This is where you'll start your quest.

Remember, this first box is just one story beat in what could be a long quest. Don't feel like you have to find all the answers or solve all your problems during this first design cycle. You'll have time to test out other ideas and tackle other mini-problems as you work through the process.

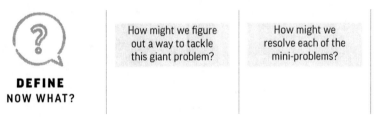

DEFINE
NOW WHAT?

How might we figure out a way to tackle this giant problem?

How might we resolve each of the mini-problems?

sxd Example

Let's look at the sxd project to see how this works. When we started the initial, one-day sxd studio, the only problem we had defined was the overarching innovation problem: empowering students to lead innovation in online learning. We already knew that this was far too big and gnarly to tackle head on. We needed to break it down and make sense of the challenge.

That's why the first thing we did was the story research, as I described earlier. Using a paired story share technique, the students came up with ten ideas or design criteria for excellent online learning to use to figure out next steps:

- Clear and concise content
- Resource-rich
- Useful and pleasing
- Social, relational
- Interactive
- Adaptive
- Saves money
- Easy to access
- Good feedback
- Learners prepared

This list of ideas—which only took an hour to produce—gave us ten potential mini-problems that we could use to start our quest. You can see that each of these mini-problems aligns with the project's overall purpose to improve online learning. We could pick any one of these and reframe it as a design mini-problem, which, if resolved, would achieve the purpose. For example, how could we make sure that every online learning experience features rich resources?

Once you get over the initial inertia and define the first mini-problem you want to tackle, you set yourself up perfectly for the next step in the design cycle: to dream of an idea that might work to resolve the mini-problem.

DREAM (WHAT IF?)

Dream is the step most people associate with innovation. Wild and crazy brainstorms with sticky notes. Engineers sketching jet-pack charging stations on glass walls. Inventors tinkering in old garages at midnight. Everyone shouting "Eureka!" Glamorous, fun stuff.

While it's true that we sometimes do those kinds of activities to stimulate ideas, the reality is that great ideas don't just happen. They don't just start on the whiteboard. And they (almost) never pop up like a lightbulb in a bubbly, brawny brainstorm. Great ideas start in your imagination. They germinate as electrical sparks in your brain, glimmers of brilliance—informed and inspired by intel and

insights—that need a conduit to the real world. Which is why story design is the most powerful design process you can choose for your innovation project.

Story design creates that conduit. It connects your imagination and your narrative intelligence to help you bring ideas to life faster than any other design approach. Here's how.

Though design as problem-solving is primarily a hands-on process, it actually starts in your head. Once you've defined your mini-problem, you start to imagine or dream of ideas that could resolve that problem. And you start to imagine how that resolution might work. You create a little *what if* movie in your mind, mentally testing and rejecting ideas, identifying bits and pieces of your resolution that may or may not work and thinking of ways you could fix them. You do this unconsciously, at light speed. Before you ever articulate or share an idea, you've already tested it out multiple times in your imagination.

Sound familiar? This is what we do when we watch TV or read a story. This is story design. Remember how your narrative intelligence works. When you encounter someone trying to resolve a problem, your NI kicks in. You start problem-solving with the hero, in your head. You define mini-problems, dream of ideas, dare to test them and discover insights over and over again until you (and the hero) resolve the problem.

That's why using story as a framework for design is so natural and easy for us—such a fast way to transform ideas into action. We've been doing it since we were born. It doesn't matter if our imagined idea is for a service, product, strategy or experience. Story design helps us apply our existing narrative intelligence in new ways, to ask "What if?" then follow the process to shape and test out new resolutions to any kind of problem through the design framework of story.

This ability to imagine something that doesn't exist—to design future stories of what *might* happen in our minds—is an insanely powerful trait. It enables us to envision amazing and wondrous things that are unlike anything we've experienced. It also enables us to imagine terrible, horrible things that we would never want to experience.

So, imagination can be a great boon to innovation as it helps us dream up new kinds of solutions to wicked problems. And it can be a great barrier because it can make us afraid to try new things. It can trigger fear of the unknown that can paralyze and force us to resist change at all costs. We might imagine an amazing new idea for innovation but never share it because we don't know if it will work.

In many ways, the dream stage of story design is the opposite of define. When you're trying to define a problem, you focus on analyzing, distilling and narrowing things down. Once you're ready to dream, you switch to more generative activities. This is the point in the process where you need to give yourself permission to get crazy and let your imagination go wild. To come up with lots and lots of ideas, in the hope that one will work. To do that, you need to let go of judgment, let go of fear. There are no right or wrong answers. Just ideas, intel and insights.

That's why some people love this kind of work—and others hate it. We all have different levels of comfort with imagination, the unknown, the bizarre stuff that goes on in our heads. I have clients who love generating ideas—and others who simply can't let go of the rules.

The great news for both groups is that, once again, you don't have to start from scratch here. If you've done any preparatory work, you already have buckets of intel and insights ready to go.

Once you have defined a specific, mini-problem to resolve, it's pretty easy to go back through your story research and search for *what if* ideas that might work to resolve it. Pick the ones that seem most promising and transfer them to the IDEAS box on the Canvas.

You might even want to revisit some of the stories you analyzed in your research to see if they trigger any new ideas. Analyzing stories about the way others have resolved similar problems can help you see your own problem in a new way. You'll often find that you can translate or adapt someone else's resolution to your own work. Remember the #campfiresintherain example. If you get stuck, you can check out the sidebar on idea generation techniques (see page 156).

On the other hand, you might also run into the opposite problem during your dream work—having too many brilliant ideas. How can you possibly choose which one to try first? The same way you figured out which mini-problem to define and focus on: sort them. You can adapt the grids and matrices we used to zero in on our mini-problem for all kinds of decision-making processes that work for many scenarios, from the family room to the boardroom. The more you practice with them, the handier they'll become.

Once you choose the dream idea you want to try out, add it to the Story Canvas in the QUEST box below the mini-problem you chose to define. Make sure you note your other top ideas in the IDEAS box at the bottom too—you may find these useful later on.

SXD Example

Once the students at SXD produced their list of ten potential mini-problems, I let them choose the ones they found most interesting and self-organize into teams based on those choices. Then I gave them a guided dream activity. I asked them to imagine, as a team, a specific future online learning experience that would only be possible if they resolved the mini-problem they had all selected.

I then asked them to sketch that future story out on a storyboard (like a mini-canvas). For example, if their mini-problem was to find a way to make all curricula rich with different kinds of resources, how would that change their future learning experience? What impact would it have? Would they learn faster? Would they learn more? Would they get more done? Would they outcompete others for jobs?

DREAM
WHAT IF?

| What if– eCampusOntario hosts a one-day design jam for students to see how student-led innovation could work? | What if–students use future stories to envision, develop and test resolutions? |

Would they have more time to do other things? Could they learn in their sleep? In other words, what would happily ever after look like for them? By working through this exercise to make the future specific and tangible, they were able to zero in on an equally specific, tangible *what if* idea to test out.

In this case, one of the teams came up the idea to add virtual reality (VR) content to courses—a pretty great *what if* idea! However, when they played out this idea in their imaginations, they realized quickly that most instructors don't have the time or expertise to create compelling VR content. Rats.

At this point, the team could have given up and gone looking for another idea. Instead, they rechecked their idea against the overall project problem: "To help *students* make online learning even better." That inspired them to come up with a more innovative idea.

> What if *students worked with instructors to create virtual reality content that enhanced learning experiences?*

Once they agreed on this *what if* dream, they were ready to dare to try it out in the real world.

Here are some other ideas other SXD design teams generated and "parked" in the IDEAS box for later:

- What *if* all institutions used the same tools and templates to deliver their courses, to make navigation of online systems easier?

- What *if* new online learners could take a prep course to help them learn to use systems, tools and resources before getting into their first "real" course?

- *What if* we could use existing high bandwidth "pipelines" in remote communities as a way to extend network access for remote learners across a community?

- *What if* we could develop a virtual learning concierge with artificial intelligence to find, curate and manage the best learning resources for each individual learner?

- *What if* we could give all VR users a test kit, complete with VR goggles, that prepares them to teach and learn in VR?

- *What if* we could provide real-time coaching during online simulations and lab activities to make it easier for learners to practice new skills?

IDEA GENERATION TECHNIQUES

Here are a few story-based techniques you can use to trigger your imagination and build on your existing intel and insights. Note that this list is just the beginning of ways to use story to generate ideas. You should absolutely try making up your own activities! You can also use many of these same approaches during the dare stage of story design as a way to prototype or test out your ideas in the real world to see how well they work.

Postcards from the future
Work in a group. Each person gets a large card or sheet of paper and something to write/draw with. You each have three minutes to create a postcard from the future (say, twenty years from now).

On one side of the postcard, you'll draw a picture. On the other side, you'll write a personalized message to yourself from the future. The picture and message will tell a story—describe the experience you're having in the future that illustrates how your mini-problem was resolved. For example, for the SxD Lab project, one student created a postcard that showed her learning marine biology via a virtual undersea lab.

At the end of the three minutes, each person shares her postcard by telling her future story. Be sure to frame the story so that it sets up the mini-problem, describes the quest and demonstrates how the resolution delivers on problem and purpose.

Random stories

Pick a topic—any topic. It could be related to your problem or not. Work in pairs or small groups. One person starts to tell a completely made-up, nonsense story related to the topic. As she talks, her partner (or others in the group) interrupts with a random word. The story teller immediately has to incorporate the word into her story and keep going. If she gets stuck, she can shout "Switch," at which point someone else in the group has to pick up the story. Stop after two minutes and discuss the story. Did it trigger any ideas or questions? If so, try to build on those ideas and repeat the exercise.

You can introduce many variations into this exercise:

- Have one person tell one sentence in the story. Then someone else tells the next sentence. Put a time limit on it so that someone has to figure out a resolution before you run out of time.

- Have two or three people act out the story instead of telling it (improv).

- Add or remove characters and new problems spontaneously.

Flip it

This is a simple and powerful technique I learned during Robert McKee's famous Story workshop almost thirty years ago.[5] If you're stuck in a rut or can only think of one idea, take that one thing and flip it 180 degrees. What would the opposite be? How can you build on that to find fresh ideas?

Far out

This is a similar approach to Flip it. Choose some extreme adjectives and try to come up with ideas for your mini-problem that fit. For example, what would be the most expensive idea? Cheapest? Fastest? Most fun? Most social? Most fattening? You get the idea. You can do this in a large group using something like a gallery walk. Hang flip-chart sheets around the room, like in an art gallery. Write one category of ideas as the title on each sheet. Break up the big group into small groups and set them up to start at different sheets. At each sheet, the group adds all its ideas to the sheet within a time limit (usually thirty seconds). Then everyone moves on to the next sheet. Repeat until every group has visited every sheet. You can make this even tougher by adding a rule that participants can't repeat ideas on a sheet. Adding constraints like these improves creativity.

Superhero swap

Working in pairs or a small group, start to tell the story of how a specific superhero would resolve your mini-problem. "What would Mighty Mouse do?" As the story unfolds, swap your superhero for a different one. How does that swap affect the resolution? Does that trigger any fresh ideas? Now, try swapping in famous people—or larger-than-life characters like your mother—and see what resolutions they inspire.

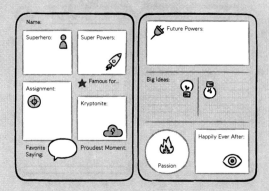

Superhero cards

If you're designing something to solve a problem for someone else—like a client—you need to know a lot about that person. Otherwise, you can't possibly understand the problem from her perspective. Which means that you can't figure out if or how your idea might create value and work for her. Some people create *personas* to help their teams understand clients better. I like to do this using superhero cards. These combine the concepts of client personas and traditional baseball cards.

You can use the generic one like the one shown here or create your own. Spend some time thinking about what you really need to know about your client in order to help her. Throw in some fun facts, drawings and so on. Most importantly, give your client a superhero name. This will help make her extraordinary and easy to remember. It'll also be more fun for you!

Role-play

This powerful technique reveals surprising insights every time I use it. Have two people assume different roles from your problem context. Give them mini-scenes to play out. For example, a surgeon and a robotics engineer designing a mobile operating room. Change up variables in the scene, such as the location, people or mini-problem, to see what new ideas emerge. Swapping roles can help too, so that each person plays each different role.

Journey map

Product, service and experience designers use customer journeys and maps all the time to reveal opportunities to improve and add value. You can make this as simple or as complex as you like. The idea is to record the steps and details of all of a customer's actions as she encounters, buys, uses and follows up with a thing (product, service, etc.). Typically, you do this to capture her

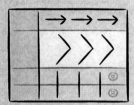

journey the way it unfolds now as a way to generate intel, insights and ideas that you can use to innovate her future journey.

Sound familiar? That's because it's another form of story research. That's why the Story Canvas is perfect for this. The customer is the hero in this kind of story. To use the Story Canvas as a journey map, you record everything that the customer does during a specific experience (like buying a product or doing her job). In particular, pay attention to the mini-problems she encounters during her journey—and how she resolves them.

Once you capture her entire journey, you can analyze it for new ideas. This is super powerful because the way your hero currently resolves mini-problems often reveals surprise opportunities for you to transform her resolutions into an innovation. For more detail on how to do journey and experience maps, check out *This Is Service Design Thinking.*[6]

DARE (WHAT HAPPENS?)

I love working in the dream phase of design. It feels like skydiving—you get high on the heady rush of freedom, adrenaline and hope for the future. Fair warning, though: making the transition to the dare phase can feel like hitting the ground—without a chute.

Dare is the part of story design where you have to find a way to get your *what if* idea out of your head and into the real world. Translate imagination into action. For some people, dare can also be the toughest part of the process—emotionally, mentally, physically. Because the truth is that most ideas don't work the first time. Deciding to take the leap to try your idea out—knowing your chute might not open, that your idea might not land—can be scary. That's why I call this step "dare."

We talk a lot about wanting to innovate. But when it comes time to act, most of us are afraid to share our ideas with others and test them in the real world. We're afraid of failure. Of finding out that our brilliant innovation won't work. We'd much rather safeguard our dreams by keeping them in our heads, where they can stay pristine and perfect. It takes a dare for us to get out of our comfort zones and subject our precious brain children to the rigors of the real world.

How do you make this part of the story design cycle less scary? By starting with small, simple experiments that test out your *what if* idea in risk-free ways. Instead of throwing clients out of the plane right away to test out a new jet-pack-powered skydiving service, you can sketch out a storyboard of the ideal or dream experience for the client first, to see how it might work.

This is called "prototyping." In simple terms, when you prototype an idea, you make it physical, tangible. Get it out of your head and fabricate some kind of "thing" that helps others see it, feel it and try it out. The "thing" you make could be a model, sketch, flowchart, 3D print, Lego tower, modeling clay sculpture or even a storyboard.

The best way to start prototyping is to make the cheapest, basic, most disposable version of your idea possible. Just like the quintessential back-of-the-napkin-sketch. Why? Because you don't want to get attached to it. You want to test it, learn from the test, then throw it away to make a better version. Unfortunately, this way of working is counterintuitive for many people.

When we first share a new idea with someone, it's natural for us to want them to love it right away. We make a personal, emotional connection to our idea. So we invest great time and energy in getting our prototype just right. Then, when we do share it with people and they don't love it right away, we take it personally. We feel rejected. "If they hate my idea, then they must also hate me." Our first response to any kind of negative feedback is to defend and justify our idea. Correct the misguided judgment of our critics. Try to sell the idea to those fools who are clearly too dense to see how brilliant it is.

This is the biggest mistake you can make. The whole point of prototyping is to generate intel that either helps you make your idea better or helps you dream of an even better idea. You dare—to learn.

We dare ourselves to do crazy things so that we can learn what works and how to do even better. Your goal during this step in the design process is to generate intel. As you test your idea and your experiments play out, you observe and note what is happening. What is the response from the user? The environment? Other people and things in the story? What is going on that makes your idea work—or not?

David Kelley, one of the founders of IDEO, explains this concept brilliantly in a short video on the culture of prototyping.[7] In essence, he says that, if you share your prototype with someone and she tells you it's perfect, that means you're doing it wrong. You've likely made it seem too polished and perfect. Or you're sending her signals that meaningful feedback is not welcome. Instead, as Kelley explains, you want to share a rough, crummy prototype of your idea, hoping that the people you share it with will say something like, "That's a terrible idea."

Then, instead of defending it, you ask them why. You invite them to tell you how it could be better. And they will. That's the best part about rapid prototyping. Humans are natural problem-solvers. Remember how in movies we all play along with the hero during her quest to resolve a problem? We do the same thing in real life. We love to resolve problems—and we love to help others resolve their problems (partly because it makes us feel smart, needed and important).

Learning to dare is tough. Because we want our prototypes to work. We are wired to succeed—not embrace failure. Yet, we must fail in some way to learn. That is the crux of design, innovation, problem-solving. Learning to be comfortable with ambiguity, not knowing if something is going to work, being able to celebrate when it doesn't. Failure is good as long as you analyze and learn from it. Innovators like to say, "There's no such thing as failure—just data and discovery."

In the world of fictional stories, dare tends to be much less experimental and more real. Heroes rarely get to test ideas out in nice safe ways like prototyping. They're usually under intense pressures to resolve their problems—now! So they just do it. They dare to try something new and unknown. They take a risk—often not because they want to but because they have to. Let's face it. Most of us are risk-averse. Doing things the same way all the time, not changing things, is easy. Comfortable. Safe.

That's why prototyping is so powerful. It lets us test out our ideas in a risk-free way. If your prototype is something like a storyboard you sketched in five minutes—or a model made of pipe cleaners and modeling clay—you have nothing to lose by trying it out in the real world. If it doesn't work, you chuck it out and start again. Much easier than charging ahead into full production with an idea for a product or service, only to discover that no one wants it. Or that it doesn't resolve a real, meaningful problem for someone, after you've poured millions of dollars into it.

Prototyping happens across industries and sectors, in all kinds of ways. Though it's been around forever in domains like software and medical devices, not many folks have figured out how to use it to design things like experiences and strategies. That's why I love using story as a prototyping tool.

Story tellers have also used prototypes forever, in the form of outlines, drafts, scripts, storyboards, rehearsals, rough cuts, improv, role-play, scenarios and more. What's cool about story design is that you can use any or all of these tools at any point in your quest to dare to try out your idea. Pick a format—like improv—and try out your idea as a future story. Improv is particularly great because you can change up different features and parameters of your idea as the improv story plays out, to see which works best. The sidebar on story-powered prototyping (see page 166) describes some of these tools and offers tips for using them to test out your ideas during a dare.

DARE
WHAT HAPPENS?

25 students travel to Toronto from across Ontario for the studio. First activity is to share stories of excellent online learning experiences.

In teams, students sketch ideas, then make and test prototypes of those ideas. E.g., include real-time simulation coaching during learning.

Once you decide what you will dare to do to test out your idea, add it to your quest on the Story Canvas, along with notes about how you plan to do it.

As you work through your dare and come up with new intel, make sure you add it to the INTEL box on the Canvas. You might also get some new ideas during this step—note them in the IDEAS box too!

SXD Example

Daring to test and refine ideas was the biggest (and most fun) part of the one-day SXD studio. Once the teams had defined their *now what* mini-problems and dreamed up their *what if* ideas, they rolled up their sleeves and started to build *what happens* prototypes they could use to test out the ideas. We provided them with simple, dollar-store materials like pipe cleaners and modeling clay and encouraged them to work quickly, throwing out prototypes that didn't work and making new ones.

Although our main problem was related to technology, I specifically asked the teams not to use technology in their prototypes as I didn't want them to get distracted by tools. We can get so caught up in trying to make technology work that we forget what problem we're trying to solve. So I was a bit miffed when, after the first five minutes, I discovered that all the young guys on the team at the back of the room were working on their smartphones. When I asked them what they were doing, they looked up and said, "Oh, we just built a virtual world and now we're populating it with learning activities." These eighteen-year-olds clearly knew what they were doing, so I gave them a high five and got out of their way!

They just proved that our hunch about letting students lead innovation was right. And my assumptions about their ability to prototype with technology were wrong. Instead of trying to control them, we need to find ways to empower them to design learning experiences and systems that work for them. We need to start being catalysts to innovation, not barriers.

The design teams all had their first prototypes ready to test in just thirty minutes. Each team paired up with another team, and they spent the next half-hour trying out prototypes to see how well their dream ideas worked to resolve their defined mini-problems. Specifically, they had other students pretend to be users and act out the story of what it would be like to use the prototype.

Through this testing process, they were able to generate their first set of design intel about how well their prototype worked. Armed with this intel, they could then move on to the fourth D of the design process: to discover the insights they would need to make their solutions work even better.

STORY-POWERED PROTOTYPING TOOLS

Storyboard

This is the easiest and most obvious prototyping tool, as the QUEST section of the Story Canvas is essentially a storyboard. This tool helps you tell the story of how your idea will work visually, using sketches or drawings. It includes a number of panels or boxes that represent key story beats. When using it to try your idea out in a dare, you can use the storyboard to create a fictional story about what would happen if your idea were real. How would you or another hero use it? What problem would she resolve? What barriers or obstacles would she encounter when she uses it? What would happen at the end? You can choose any size and format you like for this work. There are also many templates available online. Pro tip: I strongly suggest that you draw the main action in each panel of your storyboard rather than describe it. (Use pictures instead of prose.) Otherwise, you risk getting caught up in describing detail that isn't yet relevant.

Drafts

Outlines, drafts and scripts all describe what happens in a story, in varying levels of detail. You can use them to try out your idea in the same way as you'd use a storyboard: by playing out a fictional or future story about what would happen if your idea were real and what problem it might resolve. However, I'd suggest using a storyboard over a text-based tool like this for a couple of reasons. Text takes longer to generate. As well, some of us get caught up in wordsmithing and get too attached to our text. Images are easier to share. Plus, they convey ideas faster and more easily.

Improv and role-play

Acting out imaginary stories to try out an idea is—in my humble opinion—the easiest and fastest way to prototype. That's because it generates feedback and intel almost instantly about what does—and doesn't—work. However, both activities make many people nervous, as they're not comfortable acting or pretending. This alone is a great reason to do it—getting out of our comfort zones is essential if we want to exercise our creative muscles and learn to innovate.

Note that improv and role-play are related—and not the same thing.

Role-play can be scripted or not. The basic idea is to feel the emotions and sensations of going through an experience from a specific person's perspective. It's a terrific way to develop empathy and understanding while also generating rich intel about what someone needs and how best to meet that need.

Improv can be trickier, as it is not scripted and takes intense concentration plus practice to do well. If you get a chance to take an improv class, do it. It will improve your abilities to create, lead, listen, observe, problem-solve and collaborate. These are also skills that you'll find in great designers—in particular, observation and listening.

Science & speculative fiction and scenarios

These are all forms of future *what if* stories, often used by planners and decision-makers as an alternative to envisioning. The goal with all these is to be provocative: to create future stories that stretch our imaginations and comfort levels, yet are grounded in real-world trends and ideas. If you're a *Star Trek* fan, you might know that NASA frequently consulted with creator Gene Roddenberry to help it develop ideas that would advance the space program.[8]

These days, speculative fiction is all the rage, as it can help us look beyond science (fiction) to imagine and test out ideas in the future. Though both forms of story telling require more effort than a quick and dirty prototype, they still have a role to play in shaping your idea in a robust and realistic form so that you can try it out with stakeholders and clients. So, these might be dare tools that you'd choose later on in your quest, once you've refined your potential resolution.

Scenarios are used a bit differently. They tend to be "incomplete" stories, as they describe a situation and don't necessarily include a problem. (Remember that every story has to have a problem.) That said, you can still use them to try out your idea. One way to do that would be to create multiple, alternate scenarios that you could then compare and contrast with future users. For example, professional scenario designers do a great deal of research to identify trends and forecasts that they can then translate into specific and tangible descriptions of what life would be like if . . .

DISCOVER (SO WHAT?)

Making time for discover can be tough. This step in the design process requires deliberate reflection upon and analysis of the intel generated during earlier steps—as well as earlier in the process. The outcome for this step is one or more insights that inform the next design cycle and help you define what mini-problem to tackle next.

In most of my work, I choose to discover through an appreciative or positive lens, with the goal of revealing what worked well and how things could be even better. That doesn't mean that you can't cut or get rid of things. If your quest would be better by dumping your dream idea and moving on to something else, that's okay. The main thing an appreciative lens does is keep you focused on your purpose— what you are trying to achieve and why it matters.

The work of intel analysis can be as quick and simple as realizing that people who wear glasses can't use standard vr goggles or as complex as analyzing big data from a beta version of a new web tool to reveal consumer preferences. In both cases, the goal is to develop fresh insights that inform your next step.

You can use any and all kinds of methodologies and tools to do your intel analysis. Of course, your choice will be informed by the mini-problem you're trying to solve. One option is to do a fresh round of story research. This is a quick way to evaluate how well your prototype works and how it could be better. Dare to test your prototype with a group of potential users, then collect and analyze their user experience stories. Did the prototype resolve a problem for them? If it did, so what? What value did it create? What can you learn from this? You just might discover something new and inspirational during your analysis—like meeting an unexpected or unidentified need. These kinds of insights are gold when you're looking for a breakthrough innovation.

Make sure you book time for reflection on your own and with your design team during analysis at this point in your design process. Sharing *what now, what if* and *what happens* stories in a group creates another analysis opportunity—another chance to work through your collective intel to uncover patterns and trends.

When you ask "So what?" during discover to generate insights, you'll likely trigger new questions that you need to answer before you can proceed. For example, during the SXD prototyping, discovering that people who wear glasses can't use basic VR goggles made the team realize that they didn't know much about the visual requirements for VR users or the demographics of their target user. How many wear glasses? Contact lenses? Are visually impaired? Have other disabilities that would prevent them from benefiting from the technology?

Raising questions during discover keeps the design cycle going. You can use some of the sorting techniques from earlier to zero in on the insights you think are the most promising and related questions you need to answer. Add these insights to the Story Canvas in the discover section, then use them at the beginning of the next cycle to define the next mini-problem you need to resolve.

Whew! Feels like a ton of detail, a ton of work, doesn't it? It is. That's why people take shortcuts. That's why they end up with poor resolutions. Design is like fitness training. There are no shortcuts. You can't get in shape lying on the couch. You have to get up and start moving. Take action. One step at a time. And keep moving until you achieve your goals.

DISCOVER
SO WHAT?

Students analyze stories and identify mini-problems to work on.

Students generate 7 prototypes with real innovation potential in just one day.

sxd Example

By the end of the one-day sxd studio, the teams had worked through several iterations of the 4D story design cycle and had created seven wildly different prototypes of solutions to the mini-problems they'd defined. The next day, they shared their ideas with three hundred faculty members and education leaders from across the province to generate more intel about how well their solutions worked. At the end of the two days, we were ready for the final analysis, to make sense of all our intel and ask the big question—*So what?* Based on what we discovered, we were able to generate three key insights.

First, our hunch was right. Empowering students to lead innovation to make online learning experiences even better could work. Second, key stakeholders were deeply engaged. Government, institutions and faculty were all supportive of our overall purpose. Third, the prototypes demonstrated real promise in resolving some of the real problems defined.

At this point, we had worked through a full 4D story design cycle and had to ask ourselves the next question in the process—*Now what?* One option was to call it quits. We had completed our initial task: to run the one-day studio and get some ideas about how students might make online learning even better. Another option was to start a new cycle. Build on our experiences to date and continue working toward our purpose. We all knew this was what we wanted.

So we set out to define our next mini-problem in our quest: *How might we advance these ideas and support student-led innovation to achieve our purpose?* Based on our intel, insights and success to date, we quickly dreamed up our next big idea: *What if we started an sxd Lab as a virtual "container" for ongoing student-led research and design in pursuit of our innovation purpose?* The Lab would be the first of its kind in Canada, possibly the world. After playing the idea out in our imaginations, we all loved it. We're going to dare to test it this year.

RESOLUTION

As you can see, story design is neither neat nor linear. Your quest journey may tempt you to venture off into completely unexpected directions, depending on the intel, insights and ideas you generate. However, the adventure doesn't have to be random. As the hero/designer, you ultimately control your quest through the choices you make.

How do you know when your quest is over? When you've successfully resolved your story problem or when you've absolutely run out of options. (Hopefully you do not die trying!) If you get to the point where you only have one way forward, you have to choose to go with it—or quit. When you study the big epic stories, you'll notice that the hero has progressively fewer—and riskier—options as the story unfolds. Typically, she has to risk it all in the end. Whether or not she succeeds depends on the story designer.

As innovation designers, it's tough to know when to choose one idea and commit to it for implementation—which idea offers the best resolution for your problem. Of course, this becomes easier if you have clear definitions of your problem and purpose. These definitions can include design criteria—a list of features or qualities that your resolution must or should have in order to be chosen as "the one." You can try creating this list at the beginning of the project or generate it as you work through the quest and refine your problem.

Remember that your resolution is not your purpose. Your purpose is the result of your resolution. It is the impact you create when you implement your resolution, the change that will happen in the world if your resolution works. Resolutions can surprise us—often they evolve into something quite different from what we expected.

That's why it's critical to focus your design efforts on resolving your problem and achieving your purpose. If you go into the work with a specific resolution fixed in your mind, you'll miss all the opportunities that emerge during the process. And it's likely that you'll find yourself trying to sell a resolution that nobody needs. As designers say, if you're convinced that the resolution is a hammer, you'll simply end up searching for nails.

What kind of resolutions can you create through story design for innovation? Almost anything you want. Here are a few resolutions that I've helped to develop over the years:

- A documentary to inspire new federal policy for the treatment of post-traumatic stress disorder (content)

- A food truck business (service)

- A social innovation lab for local economic development in rural Peru (strategy)

- The Canada Pavilion video display at EXPO 2005 (experience)

- A strategic plan for a local police force (strategy)

- A public-sector innovation lab to reduce chronic disease among immigrants (service)

- A TV series to engage a global aerospace team in pursuit of a new mission (content)

- An evaluation report for genomic research funders (content)

These resolutions look nice and neat in hindsight. But the problems were not. Most of the time, when I started the project, it wasn't clear what shape the resolution would take; would it be an experience, a video, a service or a ___? Often, the resolution is a blend of outputs. It might start as an experience, evolve into a campaign and end up as a product. This sense of uncertainty and ambiguity is all part of the design process. The key is being able to stay focused on the problem and open to potential resolutions that emerge as you work through the quest—without leaping ahead to the first and most obvious idea that comes to mind. This is also why so many design projects fail. People get attached to their first idea and become convinced that they need to design an experience when maybe that's the wrong resolution or they have the wrong problem.

RESOLUTION
Still unknown

SXD Example

What's the resolution for the SXD project? We don't know yet! Because the one-day design studio is over, but the quest to make online learning experiences in Ontario even better has just begun. When we first started the project, we treated the one-day studio as the entire design challenge—a standalone event. By the end of that event, we had produced a bunch of good ideas. So, you could say that the resolution was confirmation of the fact that student-led innovation had potential as a way to improve education.

However, once we got to the end of the event, we realized that ideas weren't enough. They weren't a solution—they were just a springboard to another problem. Another opportunity. They were just the beginning. We hadn't completed the quest to improve learning—we had only completed one cycle, the first QUEST box on the Canvas, the first story beat in the Story Specs arc. We had only made one tiny step in a much bigger quest to solve a much bigger problem.

This is why I love the agility of this story design process—the way it expands and contracts, like the Story Specs. It makes it simple to break down big hairy problems into beats or mini-cycles that are easier to manage and resolve.

As I'm writing this playbook, we're starting the next design cycle of the SXD quest, moving on to the next box on the Canvas, the next story beat. To launch the new SXD Lab, we're hosting a Kickstart event to choose the first design projects for the Lab. Four of the original student teams have joined up with four technology vendors to take their ideas to the next level. All four are going to pitch their ideas to a larger group of students, who will rank them and help decide which ones will get funding to proceed. At the end of that Kickstart event, we'll have completed another design cycle. And we'll be one step closer to resolving our problem and achieving our purpose.

How will we decide when our quest is over? When we achieve our purpose, run out of options or die trying!

TIPS FOR WORKING WITH THE STORY CANVAS

I know that people work in all kinds of different environments, on all kinds of different problems. That's why I designed the Story Canvas to be agile, accessible and affordable. If you're working outside the box, here are a few tips to help you adapt the Canvas to your own innovation needs.

With tools

When you first start working with the Canvas, you'll recognize that it's impossible to use it for everything you do during your innovation project. Which is a good thing! I intentionally designed the Canvas to be used as an open innovation framework that anyone can use to tackle almost any kind of problem. It works best as a roadmap or dashboard—a place to plan, record and reflect on all your activities and insights. So you should absolutely use other innovation and design tools in combination with the Canvas.

With others

Design processes generally produce more innovative outcomes when you work with others—especially people who bring different experiences and expertise than you to the problem-solving process. This is when it can be helpful to try using a visual language—like icons, stick people, symbols and sketches. Design pros know that images can help you translate ideas faster than text. Don't worry if you can't draw—neither can I! Your images don't have to be pretty—just big and clear. You'll be surprised how easy it is for most people to understand a quick scrawl.

On big ideas

If you're working in a group or on a big/complex project, you'll probably find that you need a bigger Canvas. You can either print the existing paper version as a banner that you can put up on a wall or make your own giant version using the key boxes.

You might also want to organize your project so that you have one big-picture "master" Story Canvas that tracks the overall project and many secondary Canvases that you use to resolve the mini-problems that make up your overall design problem. Essentially, this is like building a website, where you have a master home page that links out to other, secondary pages.

On paper

Though I've worked via technology for most of my story career, I'm old school at heart. So I prefer to work on a large paper version of the Canvas, using color-coded sticky notes to capture, organize and share my innovation story. You might find it works well to use different colors for each of the 4D steps in the quest, as that makes it easier to find patterns at a glance. You can also use different colors for intel, insights and ideas. Or to track things that worked well—and those that didn't.

Online

If you're working online or with group members in different locations, you might find it even easier to recreate the Story Canvas as an online concept map. You'll find loads of free online mapping tools you can use for this. I'm a huge fan of concept maps as a tool for idea generation and management. They're essentially hierarchical or stackable collections of bubbles or boxes, which you can collapse or expand. The beauty of using a concept map version of the Canvas for story design and innovation is that you can make your project as big or small, simple or complex as you like. In addition, most concept-mapping tools allow you to attach links, images, references and documents. Some even enable you to collaborate in real time with your team members.

Another way to work online is to recreate the Story Canvas as an online spreadsheet. The advantages of this are similar to those of a concept map—you can make it as big and multilayered as you'd like. Depending on the tool you use, you can also add attachments like links and images. The thing I love about the spreadsheet in particular is that you can also combine it with an online survey tool or web form to use it as a research tool. People submit stories via an online questionnaire based on the Story Canvas and the system automatically aggregates them into a spreadsheet. Voilà—instant story database!

Third, at the time I'm writing this, you could use an online presentation tool called Prezi.[9] It's essentially a blank canvas that you can zoom in and out of (almost) infinitely. So you can stack or embed a lot of things into one box in the QUEST section.

The Wright Brothers

Still feeling a little unclear on how it all works? Here's one more example you can review for practice.

In 1896, Orville and Wilbur Wright set out to solve a problem. How could a pilot control an aircraft while in flight? Their innovation quest to invent the first powered and controlled airplane lasted seven years. After two more years of refinement, they launched the 1905 Wright Flyer. See if you can piece together their story by working through this Canvas. To get the full story, visit the Wright Brothers Aeroplane Company website.[10]

TITLE World's first practical airplane	**HERO** Orville and Wilbur Wright

QUEST

PROBLEM

If we can design and build a flying craft that can be controlled while in the air–

PURPOSE

–then we can empower humans to fly.

DEFINE
NOW WHAT?

How might we control the roll of a glider?	How might we transfer this technology to a glider to control it?

DREAM
WHAT IF?

What if we design a way to twist/warp the wings to control the roll of an aircraft?	What if–we build a glider with flexible wings and a control system?

DARE
WHAT HAPPENS?

Test the concept with a set of cables attached to a kite.	Build first glider with wing warping controls and fly it at Kitty Hawk.

DISCOVER
SO WHAT?

Works well! Can direct and swoop the kite from the ground.	First glider does not produce the desired lift, but controls work well.

INTEL

- Collect data on over 200 wing designs.
- No auto engine was available that met their power and weight requirements.
- No scientific theories existed in propeller design.

INSIGHTS

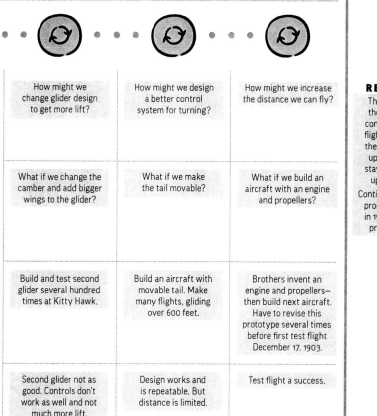

How might we change glider design to get more lift?	How might we design a better control system for turning?	How might we increase the distance we can fly?	RESOLUTION
What if we change the camber and add bigger wings to the glider?	What if we make the tail movable?	What if we build an aircraft with an engine and propellers?	The Wrights make the first sustained, controlled, powered flights in an airplane, the Flyer I, covering up to 852 feet and staying in the air for up to 59 seconds. Continue to iterate until produce the Flyer III in 1905—world's first practical airplane.
Build and test second glider several hundred times at Kitty Hawk.	Build an aircraft with movable tail. Make many flights, gliding over 600 feet.	Brothers invent an engine and propellers— then build next aircraft. Have to revise this prototype several times before first test flight December 17, 1903.	
Second glider not as good. Controls don't work as well and not much more lift.	Design works and is repeatable. But distance is limited.	Test flight a success.	

• Discover stiff twisting structure that could work on aircraft wing. Defines new aerodynamic design principle.

• Engines made of aluminum would be lighter.

• During propeller design, Wilbur discovered the concept of thrust.

IDEAS

• What if we use a set of cables to twist the wings?

• What if we design and build our own engine using aluminum?

• What if we shorten the wings to create lift?

Story Telling
An Engagement Catalyst

ONCE YOU'VE DESIGNED your innovation, you'll want to share your story for many reasons: to attract funding, report on impact, engage others in your purpose, align teams and inform future work.

The great thing about the Story Canvas is that it makes sharing easy because it gives you a ready-made outline of your innovation adventure. All the ingredients are there: the hero, obstacles, solutions, close calls, failures and final victory. You could tell your story right now simply by following your Canvas quest. Or you could spend a bit more time designing it to be sure it serves your overall purpose. Though this isn't a book about story telling, here are a few tips to help you get your story ready to share.

Design First

As always, before you can move from story design to story sharing, you need to define your problem. What is your communication goal? Why do you need to share the story? What's your purpose? What change do you need to trigger? What do you want others to do when they encounter your story? You might need to attract a funder. Demonstrate viability. Prove credentials. Inspire future collaborations. Trigger sales. Whatever it is, you have to figure out why you need to change—what problem that will resolve—before you think about how to do it.

This is huge. Because this is the thing that most story-telling books, courses and experts don't teach you. *Story design is different from story telling.* Just as painting a masterpiece differs from hanging one on a wall. You have to design your story before you can tell it. Right?

Story design is like creating a blueprint for a house. You need to know what you want to build, who it's for and what functions it needs to perform before you put your shovel in the ground. Examples of story design include scripts for plays and movies, books and some forms of storyboards.

You can't start to package and deliver—or tell—your story until you've finished designing it to solve your communication problem. To be fair, some story designers merge these two activities—like singer-songwriters, graphic novelists and documentary filmmakers who create, shoot and edit their own films. Usually though, story design and story telling are separate activities. A film director realizes someone else's script. We retell colleagues' stories at work. PR people package and present corporate stories for the public.

Why do I make such a fuss about this? Because I'm tired of seeing people like you get ripped off by story-*telling* courses that only focus on delivery. How to project your voice for presentations, produce nice slides, work a video camera, navigate the complexities of editing software. So-called story-telling courses and technologies distract you with the details of figuring out the form your story presentation will take—and never teach you how to design a story that is memorable, engaging, informative, inspiring.

Instead, you simply learn how to make pretty pictures and flashy transitions. You learn to deliver stories—not design them. You can spend billions on CGI and big-name stars—but if you don't have a strong story, your movie (slideshow, presentation, book or blog post) will still suck. It won't inform or inspire. It won't resolve your problem nor achieve your purpose. And it won't sell.

Avoid Technology Traps

Just to hammer this point home: technology cannot create or sustain engagement. It is nothing more than a tool. The fanciest camera in the world can't make you a great story designer.

My graduate research demonstrated clearly that your audience will remember a stickman comic strip that tells a well-designed story and will quickly lose interest in a technological extravaganza that has no purpose. Need proof? Disney has it.[1] When these masters of story design tested the virtual reality *Aladdin's Magic Carpet Ride* with seventy-five thousand people, they found that just flying around on the carpet got pretty boring pretty fast. Then they gave visitors something to do—a problem to resolve, a task to complete—while they were riding. An assignment like: find the magic lamp. The result? Engagement skyrocketed. Audiences can't resist engaging in a good challenge.

Know Your Audience

In communication and story design, the audience is your user or customer. They are the people you design for. You have to shape your innovation story to meet their needs, resolve their problems. This can be super tricky for innovators because the audience may not even know they have a problem. So you need to know your audience before you start to design your story. That might mean cycling back and doing some story research. It might also mean designing different versions of your innovation story for different audiences. That doesn't mean you have to change your story every time.

Rather, understanding the interests and needs of your audience enables you to choose which parts of your story to highlight and which to ignore. Think about the way the Story Specs™ expand and contract. You can choose which dots or beats to include, depending on your audience.

When we tell stories face-to-face, we often do this on the fly, personalizing them according to what we know about the listener. That's tougher to do online, with a worldwide audience. That's where online analytics and algorithms come in. Yes, big data can make you a better story designer!

Embrace Your Problems

Remember, the best way to engage people is to invite them to help the hero resolve her problem(s). As long as the story problem is unresolved, we'll stay engaged. The minute it's resolved, we lose interest. The biggest mistake people make in telling their stories is sharing only successes. (*Design* the noun, not *design* the verb). That's because we want to make ourselves look good. No one likes admitting she failed en route to producing her resolution.

Trouble is, that's not story telling. As a stakeholder, I want you to tell me about your process, about the toughest problems you battled and how you overcame them. Show me how brilliant you and your design team are—how the whole thing almost blew up and you saved the day. Invite me into your quest to help you slay dragons and search for treasure. Keep me wondering how it will all end until the last possible minute. And surprise me when it does.

Live sports does this really well. How many professional championships have turned out to be boring duds because they were so lopsided that the ending was predictable? There were no plot twists. Only the most diehard fans keep watching their favorite team long after it's out of the playoffs.

Be SURE

Mastering the craft of story design takes time. A lifetime, I believe. We never stop defining, dreaming, daring and discovering what works well and how to do better. After thirty-five years of practice, here are my top four tips to be SURE you design a great story to tell. Make it:

SIMPLE. Less is more. Cut absolutely everything that doesn't move the story forward—especially anything you think makes you look clever or cute. Remember the power of narrative intelligence. We all have an amazing ability to fill in the blanks, to make sense of your story with very few details. In fact, we prefer to consume stories this way. Leave a bit of room for us to use our imagination and you'll find we engage more.

UNPREDICTABLE. Nothing sucks the life out of a story more than a predictable ending. The audience not knowing what is going to happen next, or how the story is going to end, is the secret to making your story engaging. If we already know the outcome, or can guess it, we're gone. Keep the resolution to your problem a surprise until the very end.

RELEVANT. Your story actually needs to be about me. I need to see myself in your story or I won't care about it. That's why the best "Our Story" web pages aren't about the organization. Rather, they tell the story of how the organization helped someone just like me. When you share your innovation story, you have to show me how you make it easy for me to resolve my problem or meet my need. If you struggle with this, you might need more work on your problem and purpose.

EXTRAORDINARY. What is your X-factor? I don't want to hear about all the long nights you and your buddies spent in your parents' basement eating pizza and building your app. You need to give me something in your story that is off-the-charts unusual, unique or different. That will make me say, "What?!" That I will never forget. This could be something in the quest or the resolution itself.

Conclusion

The End (almost)

In the end, story design for innovation comes down to purpose.

My purpose in creating this playbook was to make it easier for you to innovate.

Your purpose in reading it was probably something like learning to use a new tool that would help you bring your big ideas to life quickly, easily, cheaply. Now that you know how to use story design to innovate, we've both achieved our purpose.

What's next? I suggest you take your beefed-up narrative intelligence and start to discover what else you can do with it. How you can use it to take your story work to the next level. To not only design for innovation but also to lead it. To create better futures. And engage others in your quest.

To do that, you need to start practicing narrative leadership.

NARRATIVE LEADERSHIP

Gah! Another new concept. Another buzzword.

Not really. It's more a reframing of what you're already doing, to help you put some of what you've learned here to even better use. If you're reading this book, you likely already have an interest in narrative leadership. My guess is that you are like many of my clients, a passionate leader with big ideas who keeps getting stuck. Pretty much every gig I get starts with a conversation like this: "I really want to change the way x system works—I just don't know how to get started." Or this: "I know my idea is brilliant—I just can't get my [insert target audience—employees, team, stakeholders, leadership, government, customers] to help me bring it to life."

By the time you come to me, you've tried all the tricks in your old-school leadership books. You know you need something different—and you have a hunch that story might help you get unstuck. Make sense of your complexity. Shape your vision. Engage your people. But you're not sure how it can help exactly.

That's understandable. Because most of the folks behind all the hype around story telling for leaders don't exactly know how it can help either. They can't explain the logic or practice of story telling in any kind of useful, methodical way. They don't know the difference between story design and story telling. Even worse, they often equate story telling with persuasion and influence—with spin. If you can tell a great story, then you can convince people to follow you.

That's not leadership. That's sales.

Great leaders don't sell ideas. They develop ideas that sell themselves. Ideas that you need and want. Ideas that create real value for you, for the world. Then they help you understand their big ideas. They make it easy for you to join them in bringing those ideas to life—for the good of everyone. They find the sweet spot between your purpose and their own.

Great leaders are narrative leaders. They know how to use narrative intelligence to succeed at today's toughest challenges: defining purpose and engaging others to achieve it.

Great leaders know that narrative leadership goes beyond story telling. It's the new-school leadership framework you've been looking for—the new superpower you need to lead through today's chaos and complexity. The superpower that enables you to learn from the past, make sense of the present and create the future. To study, shape and share stories that matter. To move people, on purpose.

The best part about narrative leadership is that you can start practicing right now. And if you want some tips, come and find me in Vancouver or online. I'd love to hear your story.

Acknowledgments

I'S IMPOSSIBLE TO sum up a lifetime of gratitude in a few lines. As I reflect on all that has contributed to this book's development, I offer deep thanks to the following people:

My publishing team at Page Two Strategies, for their creativity, expertise and pure book passion.

My friends and family, for their never-ending support as I veered off road to bushwhack a career path in the wild.

My TV colleagues, for sharing my journey across continents, languages and genres, to learn the way of story.

Robert McKee, for his brilliant book and teachings, which have guided my practice for 25 years.

Paul J. Zak, Kendall Haven, Michael Mateas, Phoebe Sengers and all who continue to research the science of story.

My design colleagues, for welcoming me home long before I knew I was a designer. In particular, Moura Quayle, for her mentorship in Designed Leadership.

David Porter, Chris J. Fernlund and the team at eCampusOntario, for the opportunity to co-create the future of learning.

Finally, my clients of the past four decades, for their faith in me, their willingness to try new things and, most importantly, their generosity in sharing their stories.

Endnotes

Introduction

1. Tim Brown and Barry Katz, *Change by Design: How Design Thinking Transforms Organizations and Inspires Innovation* (New York: Harper Business, 2009).
2. Tom Kelley, *The Art of Innovation: Lessons in Creativity from IDEO, America's Leading Design Firm* (London: Profile Books, 2016).

Chapter 1

1. Robert McKee, *Story: Substance, Structure, Style, and the Principles of Screenwriting* (New York: ReganBooks, 1997).
2. Tom Kelley & David Kelley, *Creative Confidence: Unleashing the Creative Potential Within Us All* (London: William Collins, 2015).
3. Joseph Campbell, *The Hero with a Thousand Faces* (Novato, CA: New World Library, 2008).
4. Denise Withers, *Appreciative Inquiry: Designing for Engagement in Technology-Mediated Learning* (Ottawa: Library and Archives Canada – Bibliothèque et Archives Canada, 2006).
5. Aristotle, "Section 1447a" from *Poetics* (Malcolm Heath, Trans.) (London, England: Penguin Books, 1997). Randy Pausch, Jon Snoddy, Robert Taylor, Scott Watson & Eric Haseltine, "Disney's Aladdin: First Steps Toward Storytelling in Virtual Reality" (237257, Trans.) from the *Proceedings of the 23rd Annual Conference on Computer Graphics and Interactive Techniques* (New York: ACM Publications, 1996), 193–203.

Chapter 2

1. Howard Gardner, *Frames of Mind: The Theory of Multiple Intelligences* (New York: Basic Books/Perseus Books Group, 1983).
2. Raymond A. Mar, "The Neural Bases of Social Cognition and Story Comprehension Annual," *Review of Psychology*, 62 (January 2011), 103–134.
3. Jean Piaget, *The Development of Thought: Equilibration of Cognitive Structures* (Arnold Rosin, Trans.) (New York: Viking Press, 1977).
4. Paul J. Zak, "Why Inspiring Stories Make Us React: The Neuroscience of Narrative," *Cerebrum: The Dana Foundation Forum on Brain Science* (online), February 2, 2015. Retrieved from http://www.dana.org/Cerebrum/2015/Why_Inspiring_Stories_Make_Us_React_The_Neuroscience_of_Narrative/
5. Start with this one: Mihaly Csikszentmihalyi, *Finding Flow: The Psychology of Engagement with Everyday Life* (New York: Basic Books/Perseus Books Group, 1997).
6. Kendall F. Haven, *Story Proof: The Science Behind the Startling Power of Story* (Westport, CT: Libraries Unlimited, 2007).
7. Paul J. Zak, "Why Your Brain Loves Good Storytelling," *Harvard Business Review* (online), October 28, 2014. Retrieved from https://hbr.org/2014/10/why-your-brain-loves-good-storytelling
8. Paul J. Zak, "Why Inspiring Stories Make Us React: The Neuroscience of Narrative."
9. Michael Mateas & Phoebe Sengers, *Narrative Intelligence* (Amsterdam: J. Benjamins, 2003).

Chapter 3

1. In *Software Engineering: A Practitioner's Approach* (2004), Pressman shows that for every dollar spent to resolve a problem during product design, $10 would be spent on the same problem during development, and multiply to $100 or more if the problem had to be solved after the product's release.
2. https://www.dyson.co.uk/community/aboutdyson.aspx

Chapter 4

1. https://strategyzer.com/canvas
2. http://thetoolkitproject.com
3. https://www.blankcanvas.io
4. https://www.ideou.com/pages/design-thinking

Chapter 5

1. Kathy Charmaz, "Grounded Theory," in *The SAGE Encyclopedia of Social Science Research Methods* (Michael S. Lewis-Beck, Alan Bryman & Tim Futing Liao, Eds.) (Thousand Oaks, CA: SAGE Publications, 2004), 440–444.
2. http://brenebrown.com/the-research/

3. Mario Callegaro, "Social Desirability," in *Encyclopedia of Survey Research Methods* (Paul J. Lavrakas, Ed.) (Thousand Oaks, CA: SAGE Publications, 2008), 825–826.
4. John Creswell, *Qualitative Inquiry and Research Design: Choosing Among Five Approaches* (3rd ed.) (Los Angeles: SAGE Publications, 2013).
5. http://www.betterevaluation.org/en/plan/approach/developmental_evaluation
6. Terry Borton, *Reach, Touch, and Teach: Student Concerns and Process Education* (Toronto: McGraw-Hill, 1970).

Chapter 6

1. Ted Kinni, *Be Our Guest: Perfecting the Art of Customer Service* (New York: Disney Editions, 2011).
2. University of Cambridge, http://www.ifm.eng.cam.ac.uk/research/dstools/2x2-matrix/
3. http://www.betterevaluation.org/en/evaluation-options/Dotmocracy
4. http://asq.org/learn-about-quality/decision-making-tools/overview/decision-matrix.html
5. McKee Story Seminar, http://mckeestory.com/seminars/story/
6. http://thisisservicedesignthinking.com
7. http://dai.ly/xjmwqt
8. Personal interview for Discovery Channel with Majel Barrett, Roddenberry's widow, 1995.
9. http://prezi.com
10. http://www.wright-brothers.org/History_Wing/Wright_Story/Wright_Story_Intro/Wright_Story_Intro.htm

Chapter 7

1. Randy Pausch, Jon Snoddy, Robert Taylor, Scott Watson & Eric Haseltine, "Disney's Aladdin: First Steps Toward Storytelling in Virtual Reality" (237257, Trans.) from the *Proceedings of the 23rd Annual Conference on Computer Graphics and Interactive Techniques* (New York: ACM Publications, 1996), 193–203.

Author Bio

DENISE WITHERS LAUNCHED her story career thirty-five years ago as a white-water filmmaker. After getting her feet thoroughly wet, she craved tougher assignments, and spent the next twenty years writing and directing documentaries for Discovery Channel. Ninety stories, eight awards and five continents later, she left the media to earn a Master of Science in design and start her own story studio. Since then, Denise has used story design to lead innovation in health, education and economic development across the Americas. She has worked for 100+ clients from industry, government, academia and not-for-profits. For fun, she races outrigger canoes, hikes with her dogs and starts campfires in the rain. www.denisewithers.com

CPSIA information can be obtained
at www.ICGtesting.com
Printed in the USA
LVOW11s1128221217
560513LV00005B/956/P